Manufacturing
Best Practices

Wiley & SAS Business Series

The Wiley & SAS Business Series presents books that help senior-level managers with their critical management decisions.

Titles in the Wiley and SAS Business Series include:

For more information on any of the above titles, please visit www.wiley.com.

Manufacturing Best Practices

Optimizing Productivity and Product Quality

Bobby Hull

WILEY

John Wiley & Sons, Inc.

Published by John Wiley & Sons, Inc., Hoboken, New Jersey.

Published simultaneously in Canada.

For general information on our other products and services or for technical support, please contact our Customer Care Department within the United States at (800) 762-2974, outside the United States at (317) 572-3993 or fax (317) 572-4002.

Wiley also publishes its books in a variety of electronic formats. Some content that appears in print may not be available in electronic books. For more information about Wiley products, visit our web site at www.wiley.com.

Library of Congress Cataloging-in-Publication Data:

Hull, Bobby, 1958–
  Manufacturing best practices : optimizing productivity and product quality / Bobby Hull.
      p. cm. – (Wiley and SAS business series; 29)
      Includes index.
   ISBN 978-0-470-58214-5; ISBN 978-0-470-93198-1 (ebk);
ISBN 978-0-470-93199-8 (ebk); ISBN 978-0-470-93200-1 (ebk)
   1. Manufacturing processes. 2. Quality control. 3. Industrial productivity. I. Title.
   TS183.H85 2010
   670–dc22
                                                    2010031655

Printed in the United States of America

10 9 8 7 6 5 4 3 2 1

I dedicate this work to my mom and dad, who taught me very early that perseverance, honesty, and hard work are just as important as education. My deepest, heartfelt thanks to you both. I love you.

A man with blinded eyes does not see, because he cannot.

A man with a closed mind does not see, because he will not.

To the first, the light is freedom.

To the other, enlightenment is a demon.

Thus is the way of the world . . .

Bobby Hull 2010

Contents

Preface

When I was first challenged with the proposal from SAS to write this book, I wondered who on Earth would be the audience. With all the very complex manufacturing operations going on in the world today, what could I possibly have to say that *everyone* was not already doing? After all, most large companies today have systems and methods certified by more governing bodies than I can name. Surely they employ best practices, right?

Then a recent conversation with a co-worker helped me see the difference. He said, "Look at all the recent issues in the news about recalls. Just about every industry, and large industries I might add, are having to recall product due to some quality problem." He went on to say, "And look at some of these very large corporations, ones who are supposedly too big to fail. They are failing because they have not optimized their production methods. Surely they have not embraced the best practices philosophy."

I suddenly realized that a certified quality system does not mean the system embraces best practices. Certification, while a good thing to have, simply means your system is documented and auditable.

Certification does not guarantee quality, only consistency. In addition, production and process optimization must take place, regardless of certification, in order to optimize profitability.

With these new insights, I understand that there is a need for a 40,000-foot overview of best practices. It is necessary to step back every so often and do an honest assessment of where we are and where we are going. I trust that this book will be a tool that helps you to make this assessment, and that as you explore my thoughts, you, too, will find a new enlightenment that will help you attain your company's goals.

As a small boy growing up in Southern Virginia, I can remember summers spent helping my dad fix up the house. Dad was the consummate handyman. Every summer, for as long as I can remember, Dad would have a pet project. It was, of course, my job to *help* him wherever I could. This usually entailed supplying Dad the particular tool he needed for the job at hand. The problem was, I usually got it wrong.

I can remember running to the tool shed to honor Dad's request to "get me a saw," and upon entering that dark, dusty place, being overwhelmed by my choices. Row upon row of saws of every type and description lined the walls, and not only saws, but tools of every kind—wrenches, screwdrivers, hammers.

There were even plows for the garden, and multitudes of different nails and screws, and boxes filled with unidentifiable gizmos. In the dim light of this place, it was hard to see any difference among the families of tools. They all looked the same hanging there among the dust and cobwebs.

"Get me a saw," I'm thinking—but which one?

Using the best reasoning an eight-year-old could muster, I made my choice. Carefully handling the saw, I hurried back to Dad's side. "That's a fine-tooth finish saw," he'd say. "But I need a crosscut."

Dad would smile, of course, and we would both return to that mysterious haven of tools and Dad would explain to me the difference between the "finish saw" and "crosscut." Dad said, "You see, while both these will cut wood, each is designed to be the most efficient for its purpose."

Now you may be wondering what all that has to do with the best practices of manufacturing. Well, Dad's understanding that knowing your tools, what each is designed to do, and choosing the right tool for the job is the cornerstone of good manufacturing.

Today, modern manufacturing is overwhelmed with tools to manage itself. In my 30+ years in quality control, I've seen countless hot, new innovative ideas become the flavor of the day (Deming's Statistical Process Control, Total Quality Management, Six Sigma, Lean, ISO 9000, just to name a few). All these programs offer some better tool to manage our business, make decisions, and manufacture a quality product.

No one system, however, can be an instant fix. No canned concept can guarantee your success. You can't purchase "best practices." Best practices come from a mindset, a philosophy developed by looking at all the tools available and deciding which ones will work for your particular goals and implementing them. Best practices also require commonsense scrutiny and must draw on the experience of your people.

Best practices also have to evolve in the truest sense of the word. Tools are tried and discarded. Some tools are adapted. Others are left untouched due to the complexity of installation or excessive cost. The outcome of this trial and error is an entity comprised of functional elements that truly works in your organization and is uniquely customized to your business. This entity is a living, breathing presence that permeates every level of your operation. This corporate consciousness becomes your center point, a place of calibration against which all decisions are measured.

I'm sure you are thinking at this point, "This all sounds very Zen, but what has this to do with real-world manufacturing, or with *any* business for that matter?" The answer is, "Everything!"

Look at any successful company and you will immediately recognize that each has a personality within itself and in its marketplace. As customers, we come to expect a certain experience when doing business with one of these companies. As a matter of fact, this *corporate persona* is what possibly attracts us as customers in the first place. This personality is the direct result of the company's philosophy of doing business, a philosophy whose foundations are deeply rooted in its best practices. For the employees, a company's personality is what allows it to attract the best and brightest to its workforce. Best practices for manufacturing, therefore, cannot be isolated to the shop floor but are indeed the lifeblood that permeates an entire organization.

The following pages are not meant to be a recipe book. You cannot *install* these pages and expect your company to suddenly sprout innovative products and break out of old paradigms. This isn't the next *hot program*. Instead, our goal here is to have an open and honest investigation not only of many areas of physical manufacturing but also of business management, decision making, and personnel. We will explore what lies behind the cultivation of a corporation's culture, to shed some light into your own dark, dusty tool shed, help you define and understand your goals, inventory what tools you have, and arm you with a willingness to consider new ways of thinking.

Some ideas you may embrace. Others you may discard. Both decisions are correct. The key to understanding best practices is the willingness to change your practices as the environment of your business shifts. Being unconsciously stuck in a paradigm is surely a death sentence. The ultimate best practice is the ability and flexibility to change, an openness to learning and exploration.

Without this ability, you will find yourself, much like that small boy, wasting precious time trying to decide your next action. All the while your *customers* are waiting for you to answer their requests. Let's only hope they are as patient as my dad.

In the pages that follow I will show you step-by-step how to examine your current methods and create a set of best practices that will help you better organize your manufacturing efforts, improve your product quality, and give you a better insight into the intricacies of your operations.

Before I can produce an item, I must determine what that product is supposed to do. I must also understand my customer's expectations. In Chapter 1, I take a look at the definition of *quality* and the establishment of quality requirements.

In Chapter 2, I address the various techniques for testing those quality requirements. I also discuss the importance of choosing the correct methods, equipment, and procedures, as well as employee training.

Exploration of the idea of inspection and its relationship to testing is the goal of Chapter 3. I also cover in this chapter the need for proper data handling and storage and how to do it.

Chapter 4 is where we enter the complex world of calibration. The need for instrumentation, which has been compared to a set of standards, is a critical part of ensuring product quality and consistency. I will show you the basics of how this system must be set up to guarantee success.

Even in the best manufacturing facility errors occur and mistakes happen. In Chapter 5, I show you solid investigative techniques to uncover the real reason behind these errors. I also give you proven concepts to prevent errors in the first place.

Having the right information at the right time is key to product quality. Chapter 6 explores the concept of controlling documents. I show you methods to properly label and handle your documented information—methods that provide certainty that what is on the shop floor is correct.

None of the chapters thus far will mean very much if I cannot control the processes that create my products. In Chapter 7, I break down the many different aspects of process control. I explain key process variables, process capability, control plans, and plan implementation.

Making changes in your process is necessary to address business conditions, quality issues, and customer demands. Chapter 8 discusses the ability to regulate these changes and contains detailed design requirements for a system of authorization, verification, and dissemination.

Our products are only as good as the raw materials and services that go into them. In Chapter 9, I show you how to source, evaluate, and establish quality requirements for your material and service vendors.

Manufacturers have no reason to exist without customers. Our customers are our lifeblood, without which all the best manufacturing practices in the world are useless. Chapter 10 examines our role in customer service and I give you ideas about customer retention, rating customer satisfaction, and creating a customer-focused philosophy.

Chapter 11 is about the care, maintenance, and organization of the physical plant itself. The physical plant's appearance and organization is the outward expression of an inward attitude. In this chapter I show you several ideas that are food for thought and that will help you put your best face forward.

Although Chapter 12 is the last in this book, it is by far the most important one. Here I explore in depth the complex world of managing people. I discuss training, mentoring, empowerment, benefits, and management attitude. I also discuss our stewardship of the people we employ. How well we manage people is absolutely the first best practice.

■ ■ ■

The companies depicted in examples or case studies for this book are fictitious. Any similarity to any company past or present is purely coincidental.

Acknowledgments

Many people are responsible for getting me to where I am today. I would like to extend my most sincere gratitude to Marvin Skeen and Charlie Jones (1944–2010), who saw potential in me and became my mentors in the early years. They are still showing me a thing or two.

Much appreciation to Wayne Jenkins, who taught me "patience" as I struggled to advance in my career, and Bud Alligood, who showed me that I could never go wrong by doing the right thing.

Finally, thanks to all the many wonderfully talented people I have been privileged to work with, past and present. Every single person taught me something.

Manufacturing Best Practices

CHAPTER 1

Understanding Quality and Quality Requirements

As a teenager growing up in the seventies, I, like my fellow teens, had a deep fascination with all things technical. This post-Apollo era heralded the beginning of the technological revolution we take for granted today. It was a time when new and exciting toys were coming to the marketplace—toys that only a few years before would have seemed like science fiction. By today's standards, those new toys would appear primitive, but during that time, anything that was a byproduct of the space-age was a must-have.

I had such a toy. It was the very first digital watch. When I saw it at the jewelry store I knew I had to have it. Despite the $150 price tag, a lot of money in the seventies, I knew I must score the coolest watch I had ever seen. Every day as I walked home from school I would stop by the window and admire the gold case with the thick gold band and the dark, blank eye that was its screen. This watch used the red LED display and showed you the time when you pressed a button. Press it twice and you saw the date as well!

I worked hard and saved my allowance and the day came to make my purchase. I was the coolest kid in town, in my own mind, as I raced home. I was very proud of owning such a technological wonder and made sure I introduced everyone I met to the latest in timepieces.

About two weeks into my adventure in coolness, I pressed the button and nothing happened. I was mortified. How could this be? It had been only *two weeks*. "It must be the battery," I thought, and raced off to the jewelry store to make things right again. The jeweler replaced my battery and we pressed the button. Nothing happened. Then I heard those awful words: "Looks like you'll have to send it back to the factory. We cannot fix it here."

Deeply disappointed, I set about contacting the company, boxing up my prize possession and giving it to the mailman. Time seemed to drag on and I heard nothing. Finally, after a couple of weeks, I phoned the watch company to inquire about when I might get my toy back. They could not give me a definitive answer. Six weeks later I had my watch back—*six weeks!* The company had now officially possessed my watch three times longer than I had. At least I had it back and I was happy.

Two weeks later, the same thing happened again. I sent it back and waited another six weeks. Then, when the watch died its third and final time, I gave up. I clearly remember as I tossed the carcass in the trash how tired and worn-out it looked with the gold case now tarnished and the shiny face scratched. I remember what a piece of junk I thought it was.

Obviously, the watch company had not clearly defined the quality requirements to build such an advanced product. Neither did they have sufficient quality control procedures in place to prevent defective products from entering the marketplace, nor were they prepared to provide fast customer service. It was their systems that were defective. My watch was only a symptom of those inadequate systems.

Today, the same company that made my watch is still in business and doing well, selling very-high-quality products. The quality of today's products is the direct result of past mistakes and improved control systems.

This chapter gives you a basic outline and definitions for quality system elements. The remaining chapters will delve into more detail about how to structure these elements, how to optimize your productivity, and how to ensure your customers will never have an experience like mine.

The fields of *quality*, *quality control*, *quality assurance*, and *quality requirements* are standalone fields. Discussions and theories about all aspects of quality have filled volumes of books. My intention in this discussion is not to write the next book on quality but rather to focus on rules, ideas, techniques, methods, and philosophies that work and come from the real world of manufacturing. While some techniques I discuss are based on well-documented and -established quality plans, other suggestions for best practices come from an experienced application of common sense.

THE END RESULT

It may seem strange to start off a chapter with a section called "The End Result." However, this is where we must start in order to understand and properly set up our quality systems. The perceived quality of your final product, how well it performs in the field, and customer satisfaction are ultimately the sum total of all your efforts. Everything you do, from equipment selection to hiring, training, education, raw materials, testing, and so on, directly affects the final quality of what ships out the back door. Each choice we make affects the pedigree of the products we produce and creates the customer experience of ownership. In light of this understanding we are compelled to embrace the *best practices approach* in every facet of our operations. This goal of high quality and mindset-of-excellence must be established, therefore, in the very beginning. Our company's philosophies and decisions are indeed guided by these end-point objectives and quality therefore becomes the core of the entire organization's mission.

However, any mission without a leader or a compass is a mission doomed to failure. Strong top-down leadership guidance, using quality as its compass, is an absolute best practice. Leadership whose philosophy is primarily customer focused: leadership that empowers and encourages everyone to embrace an attitude of quality first; leadership that understands that perfection is only an *ideal*, whereas excellence is an idea that is attainable. Producing a quality final product, therefore, does not start on the design bench or in R&D. A *quality* product begins in the corner office.

Within this quality-focused mindset, there are three terms that are typically confused with one another and often used interchangeably. These are *quality*, *quality control (QC)*, and *quality assurance (QA)*. These terms are distinctly different, but they do share a common ancestry. So to better understand and subsequently utilize them, let's explore each term in a bit more detail.

QUALITY

We cannot begin to discuss QC or QA until we can identify what *quality* means. The quality of a product is an accumulation of its attributes. For most of us, as consumers, the first kneejerk response defines quality as a matter of degree or grade of excellence. In a more practical sense, quality means how *good* something is at satisfying the need for which we obtained it.

From the consumer's viewpoint, as long as the item does what it is supposed to do, and does it for a reasonable amount of time, and at a fair price, it is of *good* quality. This definition is based solely on the emotional experience of product purchase, ownership, and expectations. When a product far exceeds the consumer's expectations, then the product would be considered of *very high* quality. This is a valid definition.

From the standpoint of a quality control engineer, however, quality means that all the defined characteristics, parameters, and specifications are within the documented limits. Is each unit produced exactly like the last and consistent with the others? The engineer is more concerned with the cold hard facts of how well the item meets design constraints and performance requirements and not so much with the experience of ownership. This, too, is a valid definition.

Design engineers, on the other hand, look to both the aesthetics *and* functionality. Does the product look like it was designed? Does it appeal to the targeted consumer? Does it solve the problem it was designed to solve? Was the cost of production in line with estimates or better than estimated? The designer is concerned about how closely the final product meets the original vision of its design and whether it does so at targeted cost of manufacture. Again, this is a valid definition.

The people on the shop floor making your product have their own set of process criteria—parameters, tolerances, and machine settings that contribute to the overall build and final quality of the product but are not necessarily a part of the final specifications. A *good run* for a machine operator means little or no rejects or rework; this is considered a good quality run. That is another valid definition.

By now I think it should be clear to you that *quality*, like *beauty*, is in the eye of the beholder. Your relationship to the product determines, for you, what quality means. Note that when I use the term *quality*, I am indeed talking about the positive aspect of the word. *Good quality*, *first quality*, and *high quality* are all expressions of the same positive attribute. So our discussions of quality shall cover practices that will yield the best quality possible.

QUALITY CONTROL

By definition, *quality control* is a system of checks and balances, testing, verification, and reactions that monitor product attributes and process conditions to ensure compliance to design expectations and internal and/or external specifications.

Our leaders have set a course and made provisions and given permissions necessary to produce the products we desire. What is needed now is a captain to ensure the ship is always headed in the right direction. Someone must be given autonomous authority to monitor and correct course, or to stop the ship altogether if we are about to run aground. This independent body is charged with the responsibility and authority to keep all the manufacturing processes aligned with the company's stated objectives. The *quality control group* becomes our police force. And having spent most of my career in QC, I can tell you there are times when you fill both roles of good cop and bad cop.

I cannot overstate the need for the QC group to remain autonomous. Your organizational charts should show no direct reporting of any QC area, or individual, to anyone associated with the actual product manufacture. For instance, the QC lab technician testing product quality should never directly report to the production line manager. This is a direct conflict of interest and simply not a good business practice. The lack of QC autonomy or independence from manufacturing may lead to internal conflict or, worse, coercion from manufacturing to overlook or bypass QC requirements so as to facilitate manufacturing throughput. So we must insulate our QC group from direct influence of other areas as much as possible.

Ultimately, however, the senior QC manager will report to a C-level executive, like the company president, who possesses the ultimate authority within the company. The president has responsibility for all areas and departments, including manufacturing and QC. If we have established the top-down quality approach, as we discussed earlier, then we minimize any conflict-of-interest problems at this level. Another must-have criterion for all senior-level managers is *status equality*. The senior QC manager must be on the same organizational level as all other senior managers.

Quality control is the central clearinghouse for all information related to the product. From specification review to process control, to final product testing and disposition, QC is ever present. Just like a cop, QC is there at our request to keep us honest in our practices. QC has the final and ultimate authority to determine if we are in compliance with our stated objectives and accepted specifications. There are times when we miss our mark, and it is the QC group who must then make the judgment about what happens next. Without QC to watch over all we do, we have no guarantees or control whatsoever of the products we put into the marketplace. Although no one likes being evaluated on the quality of his or her workmanship or performance, QC's role is vital to the continued financial success of our business. Bad quality costs money. The costs of rework, returns, missed schedules and shipments, and dissatisfied customers are all reflected in the bottom-line profitability of the business. So the question is not whether we can afford to have a strong QC group, but rather, *can we afford not to?*

QUALITY ASSURANCE

The *quality assurance group*, while a separate body from QC, performs a similar function but on a much broader level. The QA group is less concerned about specific details of an individual product and more focused on monitoring to ensure that every major subsystem is working to support the overall quality efforts. The QA group acts as overseer to our best practices systems, such as document control, process control, calibration, training, and corrective action. QA is responsible for auditing these systems and ensuring compliance to such standards as ISO 9000 or TS16949 as necessary. QA is the watchdog of our *entire* quality effort.

THE QUALITY SYSTEM

These three aspects of quality, when working together, create a *quality system (QS)* that contains within itself all of the best practices. The quality system is, therefore, the master system, the backbone of our manufacturing operations, and creates our quality philosophy.

■ ■ ■

Now that we have created this *culture of quality* within our organization, we must begin to feed it with more detailed information regarding our customer's needs, what the customer finds of value, the customer's expectations, and our ability to produce that product. Foundational to this task is the extraction, translation, and implementation of our customer's quality requirements into our manufacturing processes. Defining quality requirements is accomplished through the process of specification review.

QUALITY REQUIREMENTS AND SPECIFICATION REVIEW

Manufacturing doesn't just happen. Clearly we must have guidelines and detailed information to create the products we sell. These specifications come from either internal or external sources. Specifications are documents, printed or electronic, that must be reviewed and approved before use in the manufacturing facility. Specification review and approval is handled by QC and is used to establish *key product characteristics* as well as *key process variables (KPVs)*. We shall examine KPVs in depth in Chapter 7.

Specification review and approval *must* be completed before any order for product is taken from your customer. Understanding this sequence is crucial. When an order is accepted, we are then committed to manufacture and deliver. Realizing when we are ready to ship that we had missed a step or cannot comply in some way may cost us enormous amounts of money, dissatisfied customers, and lost business at the very least. Or worse, we may have to face legal issues for not being able to supply as promised. So, as you create the quality culture we discussed, make sure everyone is in agreement on this point. The specification review and approval *must* be the very first step in manufacturing.

Specification review begins with the creation of some system for logging in and tracking every specification document received. This database becomes even more necessary when the number of documents received is large. We want this best practice to create a central repository of all the work we do during the review step. The database also serves as a reference source to remind us that a document has already been reviewed. At a minimum, the review database should contain:

- Document name, revision, revision date
- Date received
- Document owner/customer
- Internal contact within our organization (the individual who owns the specification)
- Product or process description, if applicable
- Review due date
- The members of the review team and their approve/reject status as well as any comments
- Final QC approval/reject date and any comments
- Final distribution status

We normally think of specifications as only the requirements for the actual product itself—requirements like dimensional and performance characteristics plus tolerances. In fact, specifications also contain requirements that are not related directly to the build or creation of the product. These include items such as packaging, packing, and labeling. Delivery schedules, payment terms, testing, and inspection procedures or references to other specifications may be found.

A typical specification review cycle, therefore, requires circulation of the documents through all the functional areas for comment. Each detail of every section must be carefully scrutinized. It is not a matter of simply being able to produce the product. We must also be able to package it correctly and test its attributes for compliance to our customer's requirements. Each area then must bring its own expertise and use the tools and information necessary to evaluate that particular area's ability to meet the listed requirements. For review of the actual product properties, statistical analysis is often used. Histograms, capability analysis, control charts of similar products, and historical data help us make these approval decisions.

A word of caution here: Specifications are notoriously incomplete. Many are lacking information that we, as manufacturers, know is required to turn out a first-class product. When reviewing specifications, we must be aware of vital information *that is not documented*. For instance, if we are in the widget business, then no one knows how to build widgets better than we do, right? We know that widgets can look very similar but have very different functions, and so identification labeling is a key part of widget manufacture. Labels prevent the mixing of parts. Our new specification has no requirement for any type of marking or identification. Should we simply accept this, approve the specification, and build the product as called out with no labels? Of course not—it is best practice in this case to reject the specification and offer to work with our customer to surface the missing information. After all, who is better to assist them than we are? After all, we are the experts. So when reviewing any specification or drawing, you must be vigilant to watch for what information *is not there!*

As each area completes its review, the results are funneled back to QC for inclusion in the database. QC is responsible to track and follow up on any review response that is late or whose approval is unclear. QC then examines the results of the review and works to resolve any unclear information. So specification review can take a considerable amount of time as we draw on the knowledge of all our resources and experience to be sure the review is thorough and complete. Once the review is finished, QC makes the final approval or rejection of the specification. In the case of rejection, QC will supply feedback and detailed information on the reason for rejection and any suggestions for changes that would allow subsequent approval.

If the specification is approved, QC is charged with the responsibility of dissemination of the document and its information. The specification may be copied or scanned into a central system or simply have its information loaded into a manufacturing business system. More about this distribution process will be found in Chapter 6. The end result of the review process is an all-encompassing collection of information termed *quality requirements (QRs)*.

QUALITY REQUIREMENTS

Ask almost anyone what a quality requirement is and they will most likely talk only about attributes and properties the item should have. A better question to ask is, What is required to have a quality experience?

Or, What makes an ordinary product *extraordinary*? For example, you purchase a new car. One dealer offers you not only the car but free maintenance for life, free wash, wax, and detailing, and guaranteed trade-in on your next purchase. The other dealer across town is merely willing to sell you the same car with no extras. Which would you consider the higher quality experience? Both dealers have only one chance to *get it right* when they make you the offer. Knowing what your customers expect or helping your customers to *discover* what they expect and then delivering, or exceeding, those expectations creates the perception of higher quality beyond the product's attributes.

Quality requirements are more than just the basics. Defining quality requirements probes deeper into all the areas that touch your customer. We must address the non-obvious as well as the obvious questions. There exists within each organization a *body of knowledge* that is required to produce our goods. This knowledge consists of the minimum amount of information required to *get it right* the first time. Miss one point and you risk that very same point being the crucial one. Each company that manufactures products will have its own list of these requirements. Although I cannot possibly list all the requirements for every industry, I refer you to the Appendix, which contains a sampling of generic items for some common topics. This list will guide you in making your own list.

FINAL THOUGHTS

Understanding what quality means and the roles of both QC and QA is fundamental to good manufacturer practices. Remember that quality is an attitude and the experience of quality varies depending on how someone interacts with your product or process. You must create a *culture of quality*, starting with strong top-down leadership that bestows upon the QC and QA groups the authority and autonomy to manage the quality systems. Defining quality requirements and key process characteristics must be accomplished *before* any order or commitment to manufacture can take place. You and your team, better than anyone else, know what is required to put forth your best effort. Your *final* product quality begins with these very *first* steps. Get these steps right and hopefully you will never have a disappointed customer who tosses his dream purchase in the trash.

CHAPTER **2**

Testing

There is an urban legend that has been around for several years about the use of a chicken-gun to test the resistance of aircraft canopy windscreens to bird strike. As the story goes, the test, developed by NASA, consists of a compressed-air-powered gun that fires a chicken carcass at very high speed directly into the canopy. Aeronautical engineers in another country thought this was a brilliant way to evaluate the canopy's strength and set about implementing it in their testing procedures. Imagine their amazement when the chicken completely destroyed the canopy on the very first test. How could this be? Their canopy met all design specifications. They used the best raw materials and manufacturing processes. Frantic, the engineers contacted NASA for assistance. One line was received in response: "Thaw out the chicken first."

Humorous, yes, and of course this never happened. The story is, however, a fitting example of how one small detail can derail even the best testing method. Understanding every nuance of the testing protocol can make the difference between pass or fail. In this chapter, I will explain how to establish a testing system and develop procedures that I hope will prevent you from incurring a real-life chicken incident.

TESTING: WHAT IS IT?

Once quality requirements are established, testing becomes the next logical step in our sequence of quality system tools. For the sake of this discussion let us define testing as follows:

> Testing is the measurement of physical and functional properties inherent in the item and determination of how the item will perform when in use.

I believe that testing is the one aspect of manufacturing that has the greatest potential for controversy. Consider what is at stake. Testing allows verification that your product meets specification requirements and your process is in control. If testing is wrong or questionable, untold amounts of money are at risk. An incorrect determination during testing can result in rework costs, rejected material, disrupted deliveries, customer dissatisfaction, and loss of business. Here is one idea that must be a part of your best practices quality philosophy:

> Quality cannot be tested into the product.

Many times I have heard, "Perhaps the product failed because it wasn't tested properly. Maybe if we test it again it will pass?"

Testing a product *better* does not make it *better*. This is the reason for all the effort to ensure our testing protocols are correct for the product, our equipment is calibrated and in good working order, our technicians and operators are fully trained and up to date on the latest procedures, and robust sampling plans are in place. Testing must be *accurate, verifiable, and beyond reproach.*

TESTING: LOCATION, TECHNICIANS, AND TRAINING

Testing can happen at many places during manufacture. Testing may occur on the shop floor, conducted by operators to monitor the process. Process control testing may (but does not always) include checks for final product parameters. More often, the testing on the shop floor is conducted to verify machine settings and product attributes needed for the next process step.

Final product testing, however, typically happens in a laboratory setting under the strict control of the quality control group. Testing in the QC lab is conducted by trained technicians, in a controlled environment, with recognized procedures and highly accurate equipment suited to the task.

QC lab testing is the final call on product quality and the ability to meet specifications. QC has the ultimate authority to accept or reject production or call for rework if allowed.

If your laboratory technicians are not among the most highly trained individuals in your manufacturing site, they should be. These individuals are charged with determining the quality of your final product and are in fact responsible for the final judgment of all your best practice efforts thus far. Technician training may be done offsite or in-house, or may be part of the skills required during the hiring process. Offsite or in-house training by the testing equipment manufacturer is the preferred method when new equipment is purchased. Training on the new equipment should always be a part of the purchase negotiations. If new equipment training is conducted offsite, you will need to include finances for technician travel expenses in your budget. If you prefer to train in-house, with your own people acting as trainers, be sure your training system utilizes the qualified trainer practices outlined in Chapter 12.

Of course, you may decide to hire the skills you need by requiring proof of training as part of the interview process. Technicians may come to you with higher education degrees in the testing areas you require. These people already possess the skills needed to begin work in your QC laboratory. This is a suitable alternative, with one caveat. You must determine that the skills being brought in by a new hire are in agreement with the skill set required for the job. Every industry has its own way of doing things, and just because someone has a degree in a specific area does not mean he or she performs according to or understands how you do product testing. Technicians must be evaluated and possibly trained in-house to your methods and procedures. The skills they already possess have given them a head start on understanding your procedures and become a platform for skills refinement. No matter which method of training you choose, technicians must demonstrate proficiency through skills testing and should be reevaluated on a periodic basis.

A trained, highly skilled and experienced technician becomes a valuable resource to your process control area as well. An experienced technician typically has an understanding of *process to property*. The technician knows the manufacturing process so well that she also understands how changes in the process will affect the physical properties she tests. When a nonconforming issue arises, through failed tests, often the technician can be a vital resource in determination of root cause on the shop floor.

Here is a final word on best practices for QC lab technicians. In many manufacturing companies the lab technician is not the most highly compensated position within the organization. The highly paid positions are jobs involved in the actual production of the product itself—jobs like that of machine operator or crew leader. Salaries for your lab technicians should be on the same level as the most highly paid workers you have. For all the reasons mentioned before, the best lab technician is one who is trained, knowledgeable, and experienced. You must ensure you do not lose your investment, both in time and training, due to technicians moving on to more lucrative jobs. Therefore, structure your compensation policies such that your lab technician's skill is on par with the other skilled labor in your workforce.

PROCEDURES

Product testing is only as good as the instructions to perform them. Testing procedures must be clearly written, with detailed instructions. Testing procedures can be created internally or very often are dictated to us from specifications and other outside sources such as the military or the American Society for Testing and Materials (ASTM).

If procedures come from external sources, they very often cover a wide variety of testing situations and can be difficult to follow. If possible and allowable, it is preferred to break down these outside procedures into an internal document that extracts only the information we need and translates it into language we can understand, using terminology specific to our industry. If you have a situation like this, proceed with caution in the interpretation and translation. I recommend a team approach to this effort, using members of your QC staff and technicians. The idea is to condense down the testing procedure, removing nonapplicable information, while at the same time being sure not to exclude a vital step or requirement. It is important to note here that simply because the procedure is from an external source, the document may not include all information you deem necessary.

You will need to be aware that some information may be missing and be prepared to either provide it or seek out assistance from the outside source to obtain it. Translation of the external procedure can require interpretation. Therefore, it is best to have several sets of eyes reading the procedure and participating in the creation of the internal document. Once the translation is done and the document completed, be sure to include a reference in your new internal document to the actual source of the procedure.

If you are not allowed to create your own internal procedure from the external document, then a thorough review and approval of the external procedure by all your quality areas, including lab technicians, is required to ensure everyone understands the procedure in the same way. Follow this up with training and verification using your in-house training system.

Testing procedures developed solely in-house allows you more flexibility in design and level of detail. Just as with the translation of external procedures, I recommend calling upon the same internal resources of QC staff, engineers, and technicians to develop and assist in the writing. A well-written internally generated test procedure must address the following key elements:

- Sampling plans
- Sample selection, handling, and identification
- Sample conditioning and preparation
- Testing machine requirements
- Testing machine setup
- Laboratory environmental conditions
- Testing conditions
- Number of tests to perform
- Testing procedural details
- Safety
- Calculations
- Determination of compliance
- Nonconformance protocols and disposition
- Final data reporting

Each element listed here should be addressed within your procedures whether applicable or not. Leaving out information in a section because there is not a parameter for it can cause confusion. Technicians may question whether the missing information is not really necessary and was left out intentionally, or it was left out accidentally. So when writing your internal procedures, adopt a template approach. Use the same format whenever possible to maintain consistency. Whichever of the procedural sections you choose to include from the previous list, always use the same section headings every time in every procedure. If a particular section has no requirements or information, state this fact under that section heading; do not simply leave that section blank. In this way, all your procedures have the same look and feel and your technicians are never left wondering.

The last and most important consideration when creating or interpreting test procedures is the reconciliation of your procedures with test methods used by your external customers. You must work together with your external customer when creating test procedures that will be used by both parties to verify compliance. You cannot guarantee the test data will match when there are differences in how the test is performed. Understanding the differences in testing is crucial to prevent confusion or even rejection of product by your customer. If agreement on a common test procedure is not possible, or a test procedure is proprietary and cannot be shared, documented acknowledgment by both parties that differences exist should be obtained and referenced on any issued certification documents. Let us now delve more deeply into each element within the procedure and why it is required.

Sampling Plans

Testing cannot happen without something to test. We must sample our products in-process and after final assembly. We need a method to ensure we are seeing a representative view of our production lines. We need a plan.

Sampling plans are designed to monitor product quality and watch for quality shifts. The plan takes into account the natural variation of the process. Sampling plans for testing are essential since 100 percent testing wastes time and resources and is obviously not possible when the testing is destructive. Destructive testing is a method where the sample is destroyed in the testing process. The only time 100 percent nondestructive testing is applicable is when dictated by law, such as in the manufacture of medical devices, or when dictated by customer specification. In all other instances, taking a representative sample of product for testing is the proper protocol.

Note that regardless of which type of plan you implement, your sampling plan for product conformance should not start until the process is *running normally and is stable and in control.* If you need to test product to determine proper equipment setup or first-run scenarios, you should document a separate sampling plan and disposition protocol for these startup situations. Finally, your sampling plan should also include guidelines for an increased frequency of testing, and product disposition in the event of product failure. I will cover more on product failures later in this chapter in the subsection "Nonconformance Protocols and Disposition."

So, given no other guidance, how does one set up a plan? One of the most common plans is the most simple. For a given product produced, take a number of units or items per a set frequency. Some examples are: one item per shift, ten items per hour, five items per day per operator. These simplified in-house sampling plans are derived from your working knowledge of your equipment, processes, lot sizes, and product unit quantities. If you follow the best practices of identifying *key process variables (KPVs)*, which I will discuss in Chapter 7, you will obtain a feel for the variation of your equipment and its output. Combining that information with the statistical techniques outlined there, you can determine just *how often* and *how much* to sample.

Sampling plans may need to be adjusted over time. If you are not seeing failures and there is little variation during testing, the sampling frequency and/or number may be decreased. On the other hand, higher failure rates or greater variation would prompt increased sampling. A great analogy for this simplified plan draws on the experience of driving a car. As we go down the highway, our eyes are constantly sampling the world around us. We check the mirrors on some set frequency, watch our speed, and scan along ahead of us for traffic and road hazards. Think about how you adjust your driving sampling frequency based on conditions. Cruising on a wide-open highway with light traffic and good visibility, you would sample less frequently than when trying to maneuver through a congested interstate highway exchange during rush hour in a major city you have never visited.

Never be afraid to review and adjust these simplified plans. It is well worth your time to review the effectiveness of your current plans as it pertains to cost and reject rates. If you are testing too much, it's wasted money; test too little and the rejects or returns will cost you as well.

Sampling plans should also stipulate accept/reject protocols. These protocols show the total allowable failures per sample or lot. An example would be: *Sample ten widgets per lot/batch for testing. Accept the lot if nine widgets pass and one fails; two or more failures, reject the lot.* This is a very cut-and-dried approach. However, when the cost of rejected product is high, the accept/reject protocol may also allow for additional sampling for verification purposes in the event of a failure.

If you decide re-sampling is allowed, you take additional samples to verify your results. In this theoretical case, if two widgets fail, sample the same lot again, this time taking five more widgets. If *any* of the additional five fail, the entire lot is rejected and this is the final disposition.

Perhaps you are thinking, "I want no rejects, no defects, and no failures." I agree, no one wants these, but in a real-world manufacturing scenario, we have rejected products. There are many fine programs, like Six Sigma, that work toward zero defects and offer great ideas to help us reach that goal. Until we reach the goal of zero defects, however, we need to have a documented plan for handling defective products when they occur.

Most of us do not have the luxury of historical data or sampling precedents when bringing online the manufacture of a new product. We may also simply prefer a more formalized sampling protocol for our current production systems. In these cases, I highly recommend obtaining a copy of ANSI/ASQC Z1.4/1993. This lengthy document covers every aspect of sampling, including frequency, accept/reject rates, and guidance on increasing or decreasing frequencies. The ANSI standard is the definitive source for setting up a sound plan and is a perfect fit in your best practices quality system.

Sample Selection, Handling, and Identification

The sample you are testing is in fact the official representative that speaks for the quality of your workmanship. The sample contains within it the sum total of *all* your hard work and best practices so far. Yet, consideration for the lowly sample and how it is handled seems lost in most cases. Your established sampling plan takes care of the number of samples and sampling frequency. The procedures you are writing now must address the quality aspects of the sample. These quality requirements are not the parameters we are testing for compliance. I am speaking of the quality, condition, and handling of the sample itself. With so much riding on the accuracy of the testing we are about to do, we must ensure the test samples themselves are good representatives of the product so that our results are not affected by the sampling process.

Let's start with sample selection. Since samples for testing are to represent the entire lot or batch, it only makes sense to take the sample from normal production. I do not mean to imply we should cherry-pick our samples. Samples for compliance testing should come from the pool of product produced under optimized process conditions that are in control. Our sampling plan is our guide to randomized selection for conformance testing, as well as sampling for equipment startups and shutdowns.

Samples that are obviously broken, dirty, malformed, or otherwise not representative should be avoided. Samples that are part of a startup or last-run, or from process conditions that are not stable, are not good candidates. These inspection and acceptance criteria for samples must be documented in the testing procedure itself along with guidance and instructions for replacement of rejected samples. These same criteria should also be included in any instructions on the shop floor in case an operator takes the sample and not the laboratory technician.

Sample protection is the best way I know to address this issue across all industries. No matter the product, procedures should include protective measures to prevent sample damage, contamination, or handling that may alter your testing results. These protective measures may require the sample to be placed in a sealed container or handled only with gloved hands. Protecting the sample is the best assurance of a clean test.

When a sample is taken from the production area, it can quickly become orphaned. This is especially true in large manufacturing operations making the same item at the same time on many different lines. The sampling protocol within your test procedure must also include instructions for sample identification and traceability. The term *chain-of-custody* is useful to explain this idea. Chain-of-custody is a set of protocols and procedures to ensure we never lose the connection between our sample and the final test results. We must be able to preserve an unbroken chain from the moment the sample left the production area until final test results are recorded.

Step one in the chain-of-custody begins with sample identification. Samples must be identified and labeled the moment they are taken from the production equipment. Samples should not be allowed to accumulate without labeling to prevent the possibility of mislabeling later. This identification information may be lot or batch number, machine, operator, date/time stamp, or some internally derived control number. Depending on the level of sophistication in your manufacturing, the use of bar-coded labels is actually preferred. Bar-coded labels, printed from the same system that runs your production, ensures that all the data is accurate and allows for easier transfer of the data in subsequent steps. The key to the identification is that it must absolutely be unique. There is nothing worse than to realize your test results contain information from multiple samples made on multiple machines on different days, all of which were identified with exactly the same information.

In step two, the sample identification must be attached to the sample in such a way that prevents them from being separated. This can be accomplished in several ways, with wired tags, adhesive labels, or indelible markers. There is no best practice for the mechanism of identification. The mechanism varies by industry, product, or process. Whatever method you choose, the best practice idea here is to ensure that the identification and sample are never separated once the sample is taken.

In step three, once samples are received in the laboratory, they must be logged into a manual or (preferably) a computerized system.

The information from the identification markings is either transferred manually or scanned into a system. This log verifies receipt of the sample, when, and by whom, and creates the next link in our custody chain. We have a record of the handoff between production areas and the lab. At no time has our sample been unaccompanied. At no time, as our sample makes its way through laboratory testing, shall the identification markings be removed.

In step four, once testing begins, you will need to record results. If your system is computerized, data can be entered directly against the identification information already entered at sample receipt. If you are using a manual system consisting of handwritten results on a worksheet, you must take care to ensure the worksheets are properly filled in with the unique identification data from the sample label. In a manual system it is also good practice to have methods in place by which the worksheets are attached to or held together with the sample. The use of bins, bags, folders, or other containers that allow samples to be kept with paperwork is preferred.

Unique sample identification and chain-of-custody are our best defenses in the likelihood of a quality issue, recall, or audit. Therefore these protocols must be included in our testing procedures.

Sample Conditioning and Preparation

Depending on your product specifications, the test sample may require special conditioning prior to test. This can be as simple as allowing a sample to rest in the controlled lab environment for a specified period, or as complex as simulating field conditions like extreme heat or cold. The idea here is to be sure to include any special conditioning steps in your test procedure.

Testing Machine Requirements

Test procedures must explicitly state the type of equipment to be used for conducting the test, with references to the equipment manufacturer's name and model, if available. You may have cases where there are multiple test rigs of the same model but each one is configured differently. In such cases, the procedure *and* equipment must have unique identification information to allow the technician to easily identify the correct equipment. Procedures also must stipulate the test equipment's capability, functional range, accuracy, and tolerances. For example, a simple tape measure would be called out like this:

> Equipment required: 10 meter metal tape measure from ABC Ruler Co., Model 123, graduated in millimeters and scaled to read +/–0.1 millimeter. Tape should be capable of an accuracy of +/–0.5 mm along its entire length when extended under no load at standard room conditions of temperature and humidity.

It looks very detailed, but that is necessary because it establishes the conditions under which your testing is conducted. This information will be critical if the accuracy of your test data is ever questioned. It is advisable to also document that your test equipment does indeed meet the stated requirements within your calibration system.

Testing Machine Setup

Correct test equipment setup is vital to ensure an accurate test. Test equipment varies as widely as the industries that use such equipment. Most equipment setup will usually cover items such as distances, gauge lengths, speeds, temperature or pressure settings, calibration to known standards, and any required fixtures or probes. Each element of these testing machine setup parameters should be documented in your procedure in detail, including any tolerances or allowable deviations and known causes of inaccuracy.

Laboratory Environmental Conditions

Any test instrument, from a simple metal ruler to a gas chromatograph, is sensitive to its surrounding environment. Temperature, humidity, vibration, air quality, electrical line voltage, and levelness are examples of conditions that may affect your test equipment. The commonly accepted standard laboratory atmosphere is relative humidity of 50 +/– 2 percent at a temperature of 23 +/– 1 degree Centigrade (73.4 +/– 1.8 degrees Fahrenheit). Since each measuring instrument responds differently to environmental changes, it is important to maintain consistency in your laboratory environment to ensure the accuracy and repeatability of your tests. Stability of the lab environment creates stability in the resulting data and mitigates the effect of wide environmental changes on your results. You may find some equipment has unique requirements that call for testing outside the realm of standard conditions. These instruments have their own set of preferred conditions for making accurate measurements. These special environmental conditions require that instrumentation and testing be carried out in a micro-climate. In situations like this, you will need to isolate this equipment in specialized areas like a booth, glove box, or separate room with its own environmental controls. These environmental parameters and locations must be specified and described in detail as you write your procedures.

Testing Conditions

A well-written procedure also recognizes special conditions required for the test. These special conditions include anything outside the normal laboratory environment. For instance, sample testing may simulate extreme field conditions like deep cold or dry, dusty conditions. Perhaps your product is designed for use with toxic chemicals or industrial pollutants. Whatever the reason, simulation testing, or testing under nonstandard conditions, requires that you document these conditions and any tolerances in your written procedures.

Number of Tests to Perform

Whereas it makes sense that the required tests are documented in our procedures, we must also address the number of tests to perform on each sample. Without stipulating the number of tests, we assume one single test. This assumption may not properly evaluate our product's properties or may miss capturing the natural variation inherent in the sample. For instance, suppose our product is made from metal and has a thickness requirement. Do we make one test or several? If the piece is large, then it makes sense to make several tests in multiple locations on the sample in order to obtain a better view of overall thickness values. If the part is tiny, multiple tests may not be possible.

Regardless of single or multiple tests, we must document in our procedures the required number of tests and, if necessary, the location on the sample where the test is to be performed.

Testing Procedural Details

Obviously, this section makes up the bulk of your testing procedure. In this section you provide the instructions for performing the test. Detail is of key importance here. The format and layout for this section should be in a simple, easy-to-read style. Recipes in a cookbook are a good example. The overall task is broken down into a series of smaller tasks along with detailed explanation for each step. Consider using pictures and diagrams to provide clarity. If your procedures are going to be kept in an online system, embedded video clips are also a great way to demonstrate each test step.

Safety

Testing often involves the use of hazardous materials or instruments that have potential for personal injury. Material safety data sheets (MSDS) and instrument manufacturers' manuals are the best source for health and safety information. Your procedures must include detailed safety information and response protocols for any test with potential hazards. A good way to accomplish this is to include copies of the MSDS or instrument manual in your procedure. Hazardous materials information should include special handling requirements and a list of personal protective equipment. Information for test equipment should include placement of safety shields, potential body hazards, and lockout procedures. The safety section of your test procedure should also contain contact information for response teams or other assistance in case of emergency.

Calculations

Many times, final test results must be calculated from raw data. In such cases we need to include the calculation in our procedures. This applies even if you are using a computerized system to make the calculations for you. Systems can break down and without the calculation for reference your testing can come to a halt. Including the calculation in your procedures also documents it for verification and audit purposes. Any time data is calculated, even if it is only a simple average, include the formula. Showing the calculation leaves no doubt as to how the data is to be derived. It is also a good idea to have several people review the calculation for correctness, especially if the formula is complex.

In your procedure it is a good practice to also include an example calculation using actual data. This allows your technicians to quickly check for themselves that the formula is understood and is being calculated properly.

Finally, be sure to stipulate how the data is to be rounded and recorded. Examples of this are: Round to the nearest whole unit, to the nearest 0.1 percent, or to 0.00001 units. The rounding of your final data must follow the rules of significant figures. I recommend obtaining one of the many available reference manuals for guidance if the rounding rules are not called out in your specifications.

Determination of Compliance

Does it pass spec? This is the most-often-asked question in testing. The answer is, "That depends." Compliance depends upon a set of rules or conditions against which we evaluate our test findings. These rules are just as important as the test specifications we are hoping to meet and must be explicitly documented in our procedures. Here are some of the various interpretations of testing compliance:

- Each test value obtained on the sample must fall within the specified range.
- The average of all test values on the sample must fall within the specified range.
- The average of all test values on the sample must fall within the specified range with no individual test less than 80 percent of the average.
- The average of all test values obtained on all samples for the production lot shall be within the specified range.

It quickly becomes clear that the question, "Does it pass?" is answered only by combining the test data with rules for compliance. Your compliance rules will most likely vary depending on the individual test and product being tested.

A well-written procedure that includes these rules of compliance leaves no doubt about how you reached your quality decisions and product disposition.

Nonconformance Protocols and Disposition

But what if it doesn't pass? In the real world of manufacturing we sometimes have failures. For the sake of this discussion, we shall define *failure* as any final product testing whose data fails to meet the specification based on our rules for determination of compliance.

Our sampling plan becomes a real ally when we are faced with a failure. The sampling plan and sample identification bracket the stream of production and allow us find the last compliant data. An up-to-date and complete log of samples becomes essential in the handing of a failure. It is also important to note that, in a test failure situation, all product made since the last known compliant test is suspect and considered likewise noncompliant. Simply put, all production since the last good test is guilty until proven innocent.

We must accomplish two objectives when there is a testing failure. The goal of both is to minimize the impact of the failure. These objectives are:

1. Prevent production of more noncompliant product.

2. Isolate and evaluate all suspect products.

The first step is to immediately report our test findings back to the production floor so that corrective action can be taken. Corrective action can be anything from adjusting the process to a complete process shutdown. The action taken is dependent on your operational protocols and business rules. We must also institute our alternative, tightened sampling plan until we are sure the process is once again making compliant product. If a process adjustment is made, then a new set of samples must be taken as soon as practical and immediately tested. Any product produced while this testing is being completed must also be considered nonconforming. If your production speeds are fast and the after-adjustment testing may take some time, you must consider the risk involved in producing more noncompliant product and consider slowing down or stopping production until the issue is resolved.

All noncompliant product must be quarantined to prevent accidentally mixing with conforming product. The goal here is to unmistakably identify and remove this product from the process flow. Best practice here is physical segregation into a secure area combined with a visual indication of product status. Use of a locked cage for storage and application of red warning labels bearing the word *Nonconforming* will typically be sufficient. I have also seen special open areas set aside on the shop floor, bordered by floor markings labeled *Nonconforming*, where physical constraints prohibit the use of a cage. No matter the segregation method, it is highly recommended that the use of some sort of labeling system be used. Labeling gives you an extra layer of protection in the event the product is moved. Control of the designated area and labeling becomes the sole responsibility of quality control. No one except a quality representative should be authorized to move product into, or out of, the confinement area. Neither shall anyone but a quality representative be authorized to apply or alter any of the identification labels.

Quarantine protocols must also address steps to determine final disposition of this nonconforming product. Quality control alone is allowed to make the final disposition decision and authorize the release of the product from quarantine.

Final disposition takes many forms. Depending on your industry and products, you may choose to rework, recycle the production, or retest for alternative uses. It is also possible to receive waivers from your customer accepting the items as they are. There may be alternative end uses or markets for these items as "second quality." Quality control working in conjunction with your sales force, customer service representatives, and engineers can collectively determine the disposition after release. The last resort, of course, is the decision to scrap the production.

Once a final disposition is made, quality control representatives should replace the quarantine labels with a new disposition label that looks entirely different. For instance, use a *red label* to show the quarantine/hold status and a *green label* for the release. It is best to leave the original red label in place and place the green label over it, allowing just a portion of the red label to be still visible. In this way it is easy to see that the item was once on hold but has subsequently been released. Follow this same idea for any other labels and dispositions you may have, being sure that all the labels are easily identified from one another either by color, wording, or both.

All activities and associated information surrounding a nonconforming issue must be documented. Every occurrence of a nonconforming event must be identified with a unique incident number. Once again, it doesn't matter how you achieve this information gathering and storage. Use of computerized systems is best, but a manual paper-driven system is also fine as long as each incident can be uniquely identified and traceability maintained.

An incident file shall be created for each and every nonconforming investigation. All information from the initial test results to final disposition, as well as any retest, customer contact, or rework information, must be included in this file. All documentation included in the file must bear any and all identification data such as batch/lot numbers, production dates, quantity, and so on. You must be able to identify and connect every document in the incident file to the production run that created it. You will also find it useful to keep a master log of incidents that includes the current status of all incidents.

A periodic review of the master log can be helpful in evaluating your processes and sampling plan. If you find you are constantly having issues with a particular product, perhaps a process review with your engineers is in order. If you find the disposition quantities are always large, you may wish to sample more frequently until your process is in control.

Final Data Reporting: Process Feedback, Test Reports, and Certifications

It is a safe assumption that all efforts for testing and determination of product quality will need to be reported at some point. There are two general consumers of QC lab testing: the process itself and your final external customer.

Process Feedback

Best practices for process feedback should require reporting of the test results back to the manufacturing floor regardless of the sample's compliance. Many times I have seen the attitude of *no news is good news* and feedback sent to the shop floor only when a test fails. The idea of providing both compliant and noncompliant test results to the manufacturing floor offers our process operators the chance to better understand their equipment capabilities by seeing the direct influence of process parameters on the end-test result. Restricting the feedback only to *bad* results deprives the operator of this learning opportunity.

There are two choices for providing process feedback. With electronic systems, it is easy and convenient to allow results to be shown on the shop floor as soon as posted. This method also allows for centralized documentation and removes the possibility of someone not receiving the information. The best method I have personally witnessed was a wide-screen computer display positioned high on the wall so as to be visible from anywhere in the area. Information about quality, previous test results, and production efficiencies was all shown here in a billboard style.

If you decide that written or printed process feedback reports will work for your operation, I offer the following suggestions: Preprinted forms that create multiple copies, carbon-paper style, are better than a single form. These allow for one or more copies to be sent to the production floor while retaining one in the lab. If you desire, this method also allows for a means to capture a signoff from the shop floor acknowledging receipt. Keep in mind that the idea here is to both report information and have proof the information was received. If you design your own forms and print single copies as needed, ensure you somehow accomplish the signoff and lab retention of the feedback data.

Test Reports and Certifications

Our efforts to perform testing on final product are typically used to create a final test report or certification for our customers. The purpose of these documents is to provide legal evidence of compliance with specifications, to show evidence that purchase order requirements are satisfied, and to create a traceable custody link for quality control.

Before we go any further, let's distinguish between these two documents. A test report is simply that: a report listing all the testing performed. A certification may be the exact same data but also contains a statement declaring the data has been compared to some specification and is found to be in compliance. This one statement turns an ordinary test report into a *certified* test report.

One important note here. On occasion a customer's purchase order may ask for you to provide what is known as a *C of C*, or *certificate of compliance*. This is another name for the certification we just mentioned. It is possible that the C of C requirement appears on the customer's purchase order with no specification reference. *This is an impossible task.* Product cannot be certified without something to certify the data against. Careful order review by your salespeople and cooperation between QC and customer will usually resolve these issues.

Sometimes, however, you have to be creative. I once had a customer who demanded a certification document because his customer required *all* products to be certified. There was no specification, no governing documents, just the requirement for certification. I could never convince my customer that I had nothing to compare test results against and that without something like a specification my hands were tied. The only thing my customer wanted to see was the words *certificate of compliance* on his paperwork. After much deliberation, I finally certified that I was shipping him his product on Wednesday and stated the quantity and shipping date. All true information, but not a true certification. Nonetheless, my customer was happy. He had his documentation.

Regardless of test report or certification, you should be able to use the same format and templates for both documents unless otherwise restricted by your customer or external specification. There are data elements and information that should be included on the document in either case.

These include but are not limited to:

- Lot or batch number
- Item description or SKU
- Customer's Purchase Order number or other unique identification to customer's order including Purchase Order/line item.
- Date of manufacture

- Date of test
- Test name
- Test procedure name and/or reference to any outside procedures
- Test results and the specification range
- Data description (how the data is compiled)/raw data, sample lot or shipping average
- Quantity of product covered by this document
- Shelf-life expiration (if applicable)
- Raw material description plus batch or lot numbers (if required)
- Detailed list of cartons, boxes, or packages by identification number
- The statement of certification along with the appropriate specification name(s) and revision level or date
- Signature of authorized quality control person taking responsibility for the testing along with the printed name, title, and contact information

If your documentation requires multiple pages, you must ensure that the order's unique identification information, such as purchase order number and SKU is shown on each page. Regardless of format chosen to create your documents—printed, PDF, or website—each page of the document must bear your company letterhead or logo.

FINAL THOUGHTS

Our journey through the world of testing has encompassed a great deal of material. The task can seem daunting at times as there is so much information required to ensure the procedure is complete and product correctly tested and certified. The key to successfully creating a good test system and procedures is *patiently* addressing each area I discussed and allowing each section in turn to build on the previous one. Before you know it, you will have a completed testing system that is verifiable and clear and ensures that you know the true quality of your products.

CHAPTER **3**

Inspection and
Data Handling

My son is an aircraft mechanic. Aviation, like no other industry, relies heavily on inspection and documentation. It is a matter of public safety. Often a plane repair requires onsite fabrication of parts, in which case my son becomes a micromanufacturer. My son tells me how every job is carried out under the watchful eye of certified inspectors. These inspectors examine each and every aspect of the work, including verification that the correct parts were used and that the proper documented procedures were followed. Every aspect of the work is signed off by both the mechanic and the inspector. These documents become part of the permanent record for that aircraft and are retained in case a failure prompts the need for investigation.

The inspection most interesting to me is when they shoot the plane. When my son first used that term, I have to admit it raised an eyebrow. "Shoot the plane? With what?" I asked. My son proceeded to explain that after every major overhaul all aircraft are X-rayed to inspect for tiny microfractures that occur in the airframe due to pressure changes while in flight. These defects are so small they cannot be seen by the human eye. Left alone, these tiny fractures will cause metal fatigue and eventual catastrophic failure. The X-rays are included as part of the data package for every job.

This case study provides good guidelines for us as we design our own inspection and data retention systems. We must have sound inspection procedures, a means to assure the correct inspection is performed, and a method to ensure the inspection procedure covers all applicable defects. Finally, we cannot ignore the importance of documentation and data storage.

INSPECTION

Inspection is the sister to testing. The terms testing and inspection are often used interchangeably and are very closely related. When both testing and inspection are completed they produce the overall quality picture of the produced item and determine the ability for compliance to set requirements. In the process of painting this picture of quality, we generate a vast amount of data. This data is the evidence of the product's ability to comply with requirements and becomes the pedigree of our products. In a real sense, the data about the product is as important as the product itself. So no testing and inspection system is complete without a means to store, protect, and manipulate this information.

Let's begin with *inspection* and this definition:

> Inspection is the examination of the item for any flaws or defects that are not included in the design standard.

Inspection conjures up visions of a military drill sergeant busting a private for a blemish on an otherwise-well-polished shoe or for a misaligned insignia. How about the white-glove test for dust on your furniture?

For the sake of this discussion, inspection is defined as a visual or instrumental examination to find any defect or attribute not included in the design standard.

These defects may actually affect product performance or merely be cosmetic but convey the appearance of poor quality. Some examples of different types of inspection include X-ray examination of welded seams on aircraft, a visual exam of the paint on a new car for evenness, or counting the number of missing threads in a roll of denim. Regardless of the property or method, inspection effectively completes the picture of quality for your products.

PLANS AND PROCEDURES

Inspection cannot simply consist of randomized checks or casual observances. Inspection is a formalized process that guides the inspector through the examination. For inspections to be thorough, complete, accurate, and most importantly, consistent, we need a plan and we need a procedure.

The best practices inspection plan and procedure encompasses many of the same areas as testing with just a few changes. The list includes:

- Sampling plan
- Sample selection, handling, and identification*
- Inspection equipment requirements*
- Inspection equipment setup*
- Inspection environmental conditions, location, lighting, and so forth*
- Unit of inspection (each piece, lot, etc.) and number of inspections*
- Safety*
- Any calculations*
- Inspection list of defects or attributes to be examined
- Defect or attribute definitions and/or pictures
- Grading scale for severity of each defect or attribute
- Defect location, proximity, and size
- Go/no go inspection
- Inspection by outside agency
- Defect maps and marking
- Determination of compliance/allowable defect levels
- Nonconformance protocols*
- Final data reporting*

Several items in the list for inspection procedural requirements overlap those for testing. These areas are indicated with an asterisk. To develop inspection procedures the same considerations and concepts used for testing are used for these sections and need not be repeated here. Please refer to Chapter 2 for guidance in developing these requirements and simply substitute the word *inspection* for *testing*.

The procedural elements not marked by an asterisk, however, require further explanation. Let's explore those next.

Sampling Plan

The criteria for a sampling plan for inspection are essentially the same as for testing, with one caveat. When developing an inspection plan or procedure, take care to avoid the idea that 100 percent inspection, especially by people, can be an effective method to detect *all* defects. Just as in testing, quality cannot be inspected into your product.

One hundred percent inspection by people will *consistently fail* to detect all defects, *all the time*. If you don't believe me, try this simple test taken from the website: http://elsmar.com/Forums/showthread.php?t=1993.

Read the following paragraph at normal reading speed and quickly count the number of times the letter *F* is used.

> The necessity of training farm hands for first class farms in the fatherly handling of farm livestock is foremost in the minds of farm owners. Since the forefathers of the farm owners trained the farm hands for first class farms in the fatherly handling of farm livestock, the farm owners feel they should carry on with the family tradition of training farm hands of first class farms in the fatherly handling of farm livestock because they believe it is the basis of good fundamental farm management.

How many *F*'s did you find? Try it a second and a third time.

Were your totals different each time?

The correct answer is 36.

If you missed any *F*'s, they were most likely part of the word *of*. Our brains and eyes are trained to read these words as whole units and we find it difficult to see the separate letters. In addition, when the word *of* is next to another word that begins with the letter *F*, we tend to blend these together as one sound as we read and miss one of the *F*'s.

If your counts were less than 36 or your multiple attempts yielded multiple results, you can see how 100 percent visual inspection cannot be trusted as a true measurement. As you work out your sampling plan, be sure to avoid this common pitfall.

Inspection List of Defects or Attributes to Be Examined

Our discussion on product testing started with the assumption that we had previously defined all the quality requirements for our product. We shall make the same assumption here. Just as we must know which tests to perform, we must also know what conditions, errors, and attributes are considered to be a defect. Whether visual or by instrumentation, our inspection must have guidelines. These defect lists must be specific to the item being inspected and the documentation uniquely identified to that item. A condition or finding considered to be a defect in one product may not be a defect in another. We must therefore ensure we have a separately designated procedure for each inspection and take care to correctly identify the defect lists within our procedures.

Defect or Attribute Definitions and/or Pictures

Most every industry has its own vocabulary. These are words that may or may not be commonly found in everyday language, or in the dictionary for that matter, but are routinely used on the shop floor. Therefore, our defect list has no clear meaning to our inspectors unless the defects have a solid definition. This is especially true for anyone new to the company or the inspection job.

Defect definitions are not easy to write, especially in cases where the use of the terminology and the defect is unique to an industry. For example, the visual defect called *hole* is commonly understood in everyday life as a cavity, void, opening, or perforation. This defect is common to our life experience and is easily translated to the workplace. Now consider names such as *orange peeling, inclusions,* and *checks*. All three words are part of our life vocabulary but mean something entirely different in the industries where they are used. *Orange peel* is what surrounds an orange and is also a defect in the surface of paint. *Inclusions* could be attachments to a piece of mail but are also nonmetallic contaminates in metals. *Checks* are documents for financial transactions and are also splits along the grain at the end of a wooden board. You can see that without clearly written definitions, we are left with no guidance to correctly identify the defect.

The defect definitions in your company already exist. The words and associated definitions may not be written down, but I promise you, they exist even if only in the minds of your employees. This is why it is critical to develop a common written list to ensure consistency in inspections. It is also vital that the definitions are written well enough to cover every situation in which they may occur. My experience with the process of creating the defect definitions was to bring together a group of employees and managers to create the list together. This diverse group directly interacts with the product every day and brings their own ideas of how to describe the defect condition. This team approach created some very lively dialogue as each team member lobbied for his or her respective definition. The discussion resulted in a list of definitions that was agreeable and acceptable to all. This list of definitions was then implemented by management as standard for use *throughout the entire company* for all inspections.

You may wish to consider the inclusion of pictures of each defect condition as an enhancement to a simple definition list. The old adage about pictures speaking a thousand words rings true here. It takes some time and effort to find good examples of each defect on your list. The effort is well invested because having this visual reference removes any doubt in the interpretation of your definitions and further ensures consistency among your inspection teams.

Grading Scale for Severity of Each Defect or Attribute

Once defects are defined, the next step in writing our procedure is the assignment of defect severity. Each defect has its own unique impact on the final function or appearance of your product. As such, each defect should be assigned a severity level or weighted level of importance. Many systems use a point grade to achieve this scale. Each defect or attribute is assigned a set number of points. As each defect is found, its associated points are added to an overall total for that inspected item. The final quality decision for the inspection is then based on this total score or grade. The point system can be as simple as the assignment of one point for every defect, meaning all defects are equally severe, or as refined as assigning different points to the same defect based on the defect's size, location, or proximity to another defect.

Defect Location, Proximity, and Size

Not all defects are created equal (at least not always). Up to this point we have defined what the defect is and assigned it a severity level based on the potential impact to product performance or appearance. In the previous discussion on grading scale, we mentioned that sometimes defect size, location, and proximity can make a difference in how we assign a defect points. If this is your situation, then the procedure we are creating must contain guidelines addressing these three attributes.

Your procedure should state specifics about *when*, *where*, and *whether* the defect should be counted. For instance, a cosmetic defect located in an area never seen by the customer may not be counted toward the final score, whereas the same defect occurring on the visible surface most certainly would be counted. On the other hand, all defects that have the potential to affect product function most certainly should be counted regardless of location.

The decision to include a defect in the final count may also be based on its size and/or proximity to another defect. In such cases it is good practice to include in your procedure a numerical size measurement along with guidelines or measurements pertaining to the proximity of the next defect.

Let's use a hypothetical example from the textile industry. Textiles, such as denim for jeans, are typically manufactured in large rolls containing many yards of material. The standard production unit of measure is yards, and the standard unit of inspection is also in yards. The written inspection procedure defines each defect and states that any listed defect must be counted if it is greater than 1/8 inch in length. Our procedure also states that if the same yard contains multiple defects, only the largest defect is to be counted. If any yard has a single counted defect, then the entire yard is scored as defective. This same yard of material could have a dozen defects but the score is the same for that yard and makes counting the total number of defects in that one single yard unnecessary. This plan works fine for deciding the overall final quality grade for our denim customers.

Suppose, however, one of your goals for inspection is process improvement. Now you need to know the count of *all* the defects being created by your current equipment setup and the frequencies of those defects. The previous method of counting only the single largest defect in a yard, while ignoring all the others, does not accurately reflect the real output of the process. If our inspection plan is to include process improvement, then we must count all visible defects, regardless of size and proximity.

From our example you can see that even within the same inspection process, we can have two uniquely defined goals. We can in fact even combine multiple goals within the same inspection step. So invest the time to think through your goals for inspection before writing your procedures in order to obtain the most information from your inspection investment dollars.

Some modern high-speed production equipment creates items faster than the human eye can see. If this is your situation and these items require inspection, the use of automated inspection equipment is the best choice. The latest technology in cameras and software is utilized in these systems and can record every defect. This high-speed visual ability makes necessary the definition of defect size, location, and proximity in order to properly program these automated systems.

Go/No Go Inspection

Go/no go is another widely used form of inspection. This method is a *pass/fail* examination using two boundaries. Defect definitions, size, proximity, and so on are not needed for this method and there are no actual measurements taken. This type of inspection makes use of a gauging apparatus with the boundary limits clearly defined. The inspected item is placed in the gauge and compliance determined.

Again, let's use an example for clarification. We are manufacturing metal rods for concrete reinforcement. Our specification calls for the rods to be 12 feet in length with a tolerance of plus or minus 1 inch. We could painstakingly measure each rod as it is produced but our customer does not care about the actual length, only that the rods meet the specification, making this a perfect situation for go/no go inspection.

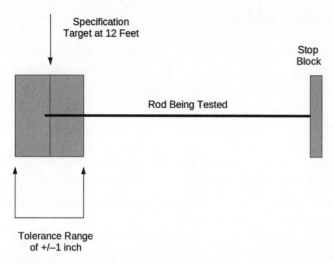

Figure 3.1 Example of a Go/No Go Gauge

Our gauge setup and use is simple. First, we securely affix a stop block at the point where each rod is cut from the production line. Next, we paint a green stripe, two inches wide, whose exact center is at 12 feet. The center point is our target length and the stripe's width represents our total plus-or-minus tolerance. As each rod is cut, it is held securely against the stop block. The other end is checked to see if it is within the green area. Any rod whose end falls outside the green area fails the inspection. Refer to Figure 3.1 for details.

So, as you create your inspection procedures, evaluate whether go/no go inspection is a viable option where actual counts or measurements are not needed. Go/no go is a quick, reliable way to determine compliance for minimal cost.

Inspection by Outside Agency

Inspection by outside agents is common practice in some industries. Companies doing business with the Department of Defense or whose products are regulated by law may be required to have third-party inspection by outside sources. If your products require this type of inspection, be sure to state this in your procedure and include any pertinent information to alert manufacturing to this requirement.

Defect Maps and Marking

An inspection to simply identify defects may not provide enough detail depending on the item you are producing and your customer's requirements. Often it is not enough to just count the defects; we must also provide details as to where the defect was found and perhaps even tag the defect with an identifying mark. Defect maps and marking are typical steps taken to provide guidance to end-use customers where allowable defects are not, or cannot, be removed. In our previous example taken from the denim industry, knowing where a defect is located and the ability to find it visually by its mark or tag allows for efficient cutting and minimizes waste.

A defect map is a written list or drawing containing the details of each defect and may include location, size, and severity rating. Once created, the defect map often accompanies the item throughout subsequent process steps, including shipment to your customer. Any marking or tagging of defects may be accomplished using an indelible marker or permanently attached tag. The marks or tags may vary in color, size, or design depending on your customer's requirements. Your inspection procedure should include specific details for mapping and marking.

Determination of Compliance/Allowable Defect Levels

So far in the creation of our inspection procedure we have created a list of defects, definitions, and pictures, if possible. We have identified severity, location, and proximity rules. We have guidelines for defect maps and marking. We even have a couple of alternative inspection methods. What we have not addressed is how to determine compliance.

Just as testing has a pass-or-fail outcome, so, too, does inspection. Testing has a specification range; inspection has a defect limit. Many industries today strive for zero defects and have programs in place to push toward this goal. Common sense dictates that we all should strive to produce a product with zero defects. This same common sense also tells us that any manufacturing process will, on occasion, create a defect or undesirable outcome. Therefore, as we create the inspection procedure, we must address how many defects are allowed, even if it is zero. We must also clearly state any special combinations of defects, or conditions that will affect the final rating. Finally, we must state, in exacting detail, the rules for final determination of compliance.

One aspect of compliance determination is rework. If a failing condition exists after all the inspections are completed, the decision must be made to determine if the item can be salvaged through reworking. Can the defect be repaired or removed without further negative impact on the final quality? Even if the defect is repairable, is the repair cost effective? The same quality control quarantine and release procedures used for testing are also applicable here. The inspection procedure should provide specific instructions on handling rework situations.

DATA, DATA, EVERYWHERE!

Everything we do in today's manufacturing environment generates a multitude of data from a variety of sources. We must therefore have plans in place for the collection, manipulation, and storage of this data. Our strategy must also include a means to protect this data and the financial investment it represents.

Data Handling

We have made our tests and inspections, either on the floor or in the lab, and now need to discuss the best ways to record, compile, and store the data. It is much easier today to collect and store data. In fact, we have become experts at hoarding data. Due to the radically reduced cost of computer storage it is cheaper now than ever before to keep every scrap of data we generate. While there are a large number of manufacturers who still operate paper-based systems, the best practice for data handling utilizes computerized systems. Components of these systems include:

- Data entry
- Backup
- Utilization and extraction
- Retention

Data Entry Options

Collecting data is not always difficult. As a matter of fact, every scrap of paper and every minor measurement creates information that can be useful. The problem we face is how to move this data into a system where we can best exploit its usefulness.

Automated Data Entry

Even with computerized storage, data collection can be an expensive undertaking, especially if you utilize people to generate and input the data into your system. Today's technology makes available automated ways to move your information directly from the measuring equipment to storage. From small sensors to full-blown computer-controlled testing and inspection equipment, it has never been easier to extract and store data without human intervention. Consider the risk involved when your data must be handled and transferred manually. Someone must make the measurement, then either key it into the system or, worse yet, write the information down on paper for later data entry. Keying errors, either directly by the technician or later by the data entry clerk, are common. Such errors can lead to incorrect quality decisions and possible product rejection. You must assess the amount of financial risk you are willing to take based on poor handwriting or mistyped data. If, during your review of quality requirements and budget, you find new instruments are needed, consider those that allow for this automated download. The added cost of these instruments is soon regained through increased efficiency, cleanliness of the data stream, and the assurance that you are getting the best data for your quality conformance determination.

If your testing and inspection areas are already well established and automation is not possible at this time, you can benefit from a review of how you are currently moving your data to storage. It is always the best practice to periodically review your methods and data handling. For instance, when you have technicians performing a test, how is the data recorded? As mentioned earlier, the worse case is where the data is written down and later keyed into storage by someone other than the technicians themselves. The data in this case is handled at least twice and each handling increases the likelihood of errors through transposition or misreading. If this is how you currently handle your data entry, I offer one suggestion for improvement. Set up the data entry screens to show the specification ranges. Then program the system to compare the entry to the required ranges for compliance. Even simple spreadsheets can be set up to perform these functions. This method will, at the very least, highlight keying errors for correction or allow faster feedback to technicians for follow-up and feedback to production.

Direct Data Entry

If your equipment is not and cannot be automated, then the next best option is to allow technicians to directly enter data using an access point at each workstation. This access point can be as simple as a standalone PC or as complex as hand-held wireless units connected to a centralized server. No matter the equipment, directly entering the data removes one layer of uncertainty by removing the *written* recording and data clerk step. If you also implement the data-check-and-verify routine mentioned earlier, you have a very good chance of keeping your data clean and, more importantly, accurate.

Scanning Documents

If your facilities are still mostly paper based, it is safe to assume there are great challenges in filing, accessing, and storing all that paperwork. A simple, economical solution is the purchase of a PC with a document scanner and printer. As paperwork comes in, first organize it into natural groups such as order number, lot/batch, or date. Then scan the documents and save them in a computer folder with the appropriate identification. Once done, the paper may be discarded for recycling. Your documents are now at your fingertips if needed and organized for easy retrieval. The storage space cost savings alone would quickly offset the cost of the PC and associated equipment.

Obviously this is not the method of choice, as your data cannot be analyzed or manipulated with computer software, but *best practices are those that are the best you can afford*. So small improvements are still improvements and improvement is definitely the best practice.

Backup

Now that we have a computerized system in place, there is a required best practice that is an absolute must. You *must* create a backup of all your data, at least every day. To *back up* means to create another copy of all your information for storage away from your main manufacturing site in a safe location. As we all know, computers are prone to failures, viruses, and a host of other maladies. While the computer has changed how we manage our data, it also keeps us only one virus away from total destruction. In addition, in a manufacturing environment there is always the threat of industrial accident or fire, as well as acts of nature. Common sense dictates that a backup of your data should be kept somewhere other than the site where it is generated. The storage should be in a fireproof safe within a controlled environment. Another backup alternative is mirrored transactions. This choice duplicates the information received by your main computer system and stores it in another remote location, in real time, on a sister system. In the event of a disaster or failure, the mirrored system can be back online quickly and is up to date as of the last transaction, making this method the best practice for backups.

One last note on backups: *Your backup is only as good as your ability to retrieve and restore the data.* Create a disaster recovery plan and test it at least once a year. You do not want to wait until you need to restore data, only to find it impossible.

With great ability comes great responsibility. Back up your data regularly. All computer systems today have a means to put these backup routines on an automated schedule. You must decide as you implement your system just how much information you can afford to lose or recreate if lost and schedule the backup accordingly. Just remember, back it up!

Data Utilization and Extraction

Regardless of which electronic data collection and storage option you choose, information that is difficult or impossible to access is worthless. Information silos are created when access is limited by being housed on a standalone PC or by having poorly designed databases that take a long time to open and process. We want to avoid the situation of having a solitary person *in charge* of the data that is located on a single user PC. This *go-to* person is the only one who can access, extract, and manipulate the information. The business and manufacturing world of today moves with such speed that information has to be accessible instantly and easily by the end users. Gone is the day where the Information Technology group is the sole source of information and we can afford to wait days for a report to be created.

The best designed information systems are server based and act as the central repository for the data, the software, and the programs for analysis and reporting. We then provide a simple browser-based portal to the end user to display the final report content from the server. This method allows delivery of polished summarized data to any devices that are browser compatible, such as smart phones, PDAs, and net-books. Server-based solutions to data storage, retrieval, and manipulation free us from the data silos of the past and put the power of the information at our users' fingertips where it is most useful.

Return on the investment of data collection and storage is another reason to move away from data silos to data warehouses that are easy to access. Consider what it costs your company to sample product, test it, enter the data into whatever system you choose, and store it there.

As an example, let us assign one dollar per data point. This one-dollar value includes the sample cost, the labor to produce the sample, overhead, technician wages, benefits, perhaps even clerks to key in the data. Now suppose you conduct testing on large numbers of samples over many years. This investment can quickly reach into thousands, if not millions, of dollars invested, just collecting data. Therefore, the data has just as much real financial value as any part of your physical plant or machinery. Yet, for most companies, once the data is collected it is used for either product certifications or process control, and is tucked away never to be seen again, unless some issue arises that warrants its retrieval.

Now consider this: Would you be happy to invest this amount of financial resources into any other area of your business and receive absolutely no return? Certainly not—the data you collect can be used to guide your business decisions and provide a window into process performance. Statistical analysis using tools like control charts, histograms, and process capability can show trends, shifts, multiple populations, and process variations using data already collected. A small percentage of the data's value invested into analytical software allows you to mine the wealth from money already spent and certainly gives you a better return on investment than simple storage alone.

Data Retention

The final component of data handling involves data retention times. While electronic storage allows data to be kept live and online indefinitely, this may not be practical. Typical storage time for most manufacturing information and/or documents is seven to ten years unless otherwise dictated by law or customer specification. Retention time may also differ depending on the data type. For example, customer order data may be kept longer than purchase order information. Therefore, it is the best practice to document the retention time for each data type in a published procedure. This documented procedure then stands in evidence should the removal of certain data ever come into question.

FINAL THOUGHTS

Developing an inspection plan involves many of the same aspects and thought processes as testing. These common elements, combined with the special inspection requirements we have discussed, create the best practices inspection system—an inspection system with the sensitivity to capture and report defects and provide final disposition. By combining our inspection and testing systems we build for ourselves a complete set of tools to evaluate our product quality—tools that allow us to monitor both process and product, tools that give us confidence that our customers will have the positive quality experience we want them to have.

The modern world is drenched in data. In manufacturing we must be able to react, be more innovative, and move faster than our competition. We cannot achieve this by basing our decisions on speculation or guesswork. We must *know*. We must first generate and then utilize all the data possible in our decision-making process. We also have to ensure the data is both accurate and precise. With competition so fierce, we have no choice but to create a data-driven business if we are to survive. While this takes forethought and investment, information has become the lifeblood of modern manufacturing.

CHAPTER **4**

Calibration

The Holdfast Nut and Bolt Company has been in business since 1897. This company, which has supplied various fastening devices to a broad spectrum of industries, has cause for celebration. It was recently awarded its first government contract to supply bolts to the Department of Defense for use in its newest fleet of ground vehicles. Holdfast was chosen because of its high quality and lowest price.

The order quantities were large, even by Holdfast standards. The order was for 500,000 bolt-and-nut packages. The specification called for the highest grade, most expensive steel available and various heat treatments. The tolerances were the tightest Holdfast had ever seen. This was the most complex job Holdfast had undertaken in its history and the end product had the highest production cost of any product thus far. In spite of this, the company felt up to the challenge.

Due to the importance of the order, Holdfast placed only its most senior and experienced operators on the project. The big day came when the first batch of 5,000 were ready for final inspection and acceptance by the government inspector. To everyone's horror, the bolts were too short by less than a millimeter. How on earth could this happen? There was a calibration system in place and every tool was checked before production started. This one batch cost thousands of dollars to produce and now it was out of specification and there was no way to repair it.

An investigation ensued and the cause was soon found. The senior machinist who cut the bolts to length was the sixth generation of his family to work for Holdfast. He took great pride in that fact and also in the fact that his tools of the trade were handed down through the generations of machinists before him. The calipers he used to set up his equipment belonged to his great-grandfather and as such were always kept in a special, safe place in his toolbox and used only for special jobs.

Unfortunately, those calipers had not been calibrated in the many decades since his ancestor owned them. Indeed, due to their age and design, the calipers would not have been accurate enough for the task even if they were calibrated. The machinist, with no malicious intention, had kept his special tools out of the company's calibration system. This was a decision that cost the company dearly—not only financially but, more so, in reputation.

Of course, this story is fictional. Common sense would dictate that a senior machinist would know his tools must be calibrated. As managers of our systems, however, we cannot trust that common sense prevails. We must have systems that identify every gauge and instrument we use for measurements. We must educate our employees about the importance of using only calibrated tools and we must verify on a regular basis that our system is sound.

Calibration is a detailed science in its own right and many fine books and courses are available to teach you the details. Each instrument type and required resolution will require different calibration methods and standards. With so many possible different scenarios and the complexity involved with calibration, it is not within the scope of this chapter to be a definitive source for specific details for every situation. What I hope to achieve is to introduce you to the basic ideas and concepts surrounding calibration and why it is a required part of your best practices toolkit.

I have already established that you must take every precaution possible to ensure your testing methods and results are indisputable. A robust calibration system is a cornerstone to achieving this objective. You may have all the very best equipment money can buy, perfectly well-written procedures, and a state-of-the-art laboratory with technicians possessing a Ph.D. in their field, but without a means to calibrate your instruments you may as well use sticks and rocks for measuring or simply make up your results.

In a layperson's terms, calibration is the act of comparing the measurement output of an instrument to a known standard. How do you know a 12-inch ruler is exactly 12 inches long? You don't. How sure are you that the air-pressure gauge you use to inflate your tires is correct when it says 32 psi? The short answer is that you are not sure. You can be certain only that all measurements are uncertain unless the instrument has been calibrated on a regular basis and there is traceable evidence to a known standard.

There are many parts to a robust calibration system and several decisions you will need to make in setting up your system. Let's touch on each one.

GAUGE IDENTIFICATION

For the sake of this discussion, a gauge is any instrument capable of making a measurement.

Most manufacturing operations utilize many different types of gauges or many of the same gauges throughout the shop floor. Uniquely identifying each gauge is the first and most vital link in our chain. The identification terminology you use does not really matter. You can use names or numbers or any other marking you prefer. However, the identification you use must be *absolutely unique* to that single gauge, *forever*. A well-designed calibration system does not allow for the duplication or recycling of identification. Once an identification is assigned, it is never used again.

The best method to prevent errors of this nature is to use a computerized management system that creates the identification for you based on your identification rules. It has been my experience that a simple numbering system is sufficient, allowing the system to assign the next number in sequence for a new gauge. Any additional specific details about the gauge can be easily stored along with the identification number.

Now that we have our identification sorted out we need to be sure our gauge is properly tagged. In most situations gauges can have a permanent tag attached and this is preferred. I suggest using tags that are not susceptible to wear, and cannot be easily removed. Stick-on labels and tape are not preferred. Metal tags attached with fasteners are a good choice. Engraving and etching are also useful for permanent identification. If you cannot use any of these methods and must resort to using a label that is more susceptible to damage, take precautions to use the most robust labels you can find. For example, stick-on labels made from metal foil are a much better choice than paper. Once applied, take steps to ensure the label is protected from damage. Coating with a clear sealant or covering with a transparent plastic covering are good choices.

If the gauge is used in harsh environmental conditions, choose whatever labeling and protection method affords the best chance of survival for the identification marks. The key here is to prevent the separation of the gauge from its identification for the life of the gauge. If the identification is lost, then traceability is lost.

In addition to the identification tags, each gauge must bear an additional tag that indicates its calibration status. A minimum of three pieces of information must be included on this tag: *the date of the last calibration, the due date of the next calibration,* and *by whom the calibration was performed.* In this way, anyone who uses a particular gauge can tell at a glance that the gauge can be used. You should also include in your employee work instructions and test procedures the requirement to verify that the gauge calibration is current and not out of date. These date tags require the same durability as the identification tags but must be able to be removed, replaced, or updated to reflect the current calibration status.

One important note on tagging: All of the suggestions given previously assume the tagging and label will *not* affect the gauge functionality. Do not attach any tags to instruments if the tag will interfere in any way with the accuracy of the gauge. Items like weights, for instance, cannot have tags attached or be engraved as this would add or remove weight, respectively. A ruler, for example, may not be able to be read with a tag obscuring its face. Most manufacturers of this type of gauge recognize the problem in identifying items like these and will incorporate a serial number into the gauge itself during manufacture. This manufacturer's serial number can be used in your system, along with your own internal identification for cross reference. If the gauge does not come already labeled, and cannot be labeled without affecting its measurements, the best you can do is to label the container holding the gauge or place the identification as close to the gauge as possible.

A final word on identification labeling: There will be times when you have an instrument that is capable of making measurements but is not utilized in any testing procedures. A good example is the clock on the wall. It marks off time, usually to the second, and is there simply for reference to the time of day. The same clock, however, could be used to time a test versus a calibrated watch. It is good practice then to label the wall clock, and any other instrument that is not to be used, with a label stating NOT CALIBRATED or CALIBRATION NOT REQUIRED. This makes it clear to everyone that the instrument is there for reference only and is not to be used for making final determinations. In this way every gauge or instrument in your facility is clearly marked as to its function, avoiding confusion and potential errors in testing.

CALIBRATION STANDARDS

Your calibrations are only as good as the standards used to perform them. All standards must be traceable, with an unbroken chain, back to a master standard certified by some governing body. Typically, in the United States, this governing body is the National Institute of Standards and Technology (NIST). There are equivalent agencies like this in most other countries. NIST can provide or certify a set of measurement standards for every type of measurement device based on calibrations performed against NIST master standards. NIST provides these standards and certifications to companies that will in turn produce standards for use in industry.

Standards used for calibrations must be more accurate than the instrument being calibrated. The generally recognized accuracy ratio is 4:1. This means that the standard you choose should be four times more accurate than the instrument being calibrated. For instance, a scale that measures to +/–1 gram should be calibrated with a standard weight accurate to +/–0.0001 grams. This same ratio applies upstream throughout the traceability chain. Each master standard itself is calibrated by standards with increasingly higher levels of accuracy. With today's technology and instruments capable of higher and higher degrees of accuracy, it is difficult to maintain the 4:1 ratio as the ratio becomes impractical or impossible. The best practical rule of thumb is to ensure your standards are more accurate than the instrument being calibrated.

Great care must be exercised in the handling of your standards. The first and most important rule is that standards are never to be used for actual product testing or equipment setup. Standards are used only for the purposes of calibration. When not in use, your standards should be kept in a secure place with limited access by only those authorized to perform the calibrations. Protection of the standards is crucial to maintain their accuracy. Electronic standards should be kept in a stable environment and protected from static electricity. For physical standards such as metal rulers, gauge blocks, or weights, care must be taken to store these to prevent rust or corrosion, which will affect the accuracy of the standard. In addition, a physical standard should never be touched by bare hands when being used. Gloves should be worn at all times or the standard handled with instruments like tweezers. The oils from your hands are extremely corrosive and will damage your standards.

Standards must also be uniquely identified and included in your calibration system. Standards are treated like every other gauge as they themselves must be calibrated on a regular frequency. Remember your standards are your assurance that the testing gauge is correct and your data is sound.

CALIBRATION RECALL AND DATA MANAGEMENT SYSTEM

Your calibration plan is centralized around the recall and data management system. This system most assuredly should be computerized. This is especially true when there are a large number of gauges in use. As we shall see in the following paragraphs, there are many pieces of data that should be kept and a strong need for an easily managed recall system.

What exactly is a recall system? Recall is the heart of the calibration system. Recall is the ability to identify all gauges coming due for calibration during a given time period and being able to locate and retrieve those gauges. The goal here is to identify and calibrate the gauges *before* the next due date. Recall systems need only contain the gauge identification, calibration frequency, and its next calibration date. Putting this data in a computer allows for quick querying of the information and accurate accounting for all the due gauges.

Recall systems are based on a frequency determined internally by your operational needs, as dictated by the gauge manufacturer, or as outlined in a specification. A manageable frequency is monthly. That is not to say every gauge is to be checked every month. A monthly frequency unit means our system is based on months and not weeks, days, or years. A gauge may be checked every 3 months, 6 months, 12 months, and so on, but *months* is our unit of measure. Having a standardized frequency unit simplifies the system but you can certainly have multiple frequency units if needed.

Although the recall system can be as simple as a database with gauge identification, frequency, and due date, it is a good practice to incorporate as much information into our database as possible. Doing so will help us facilitate record keeping, traceability, and calibration procedures, and make the calibration process more efficient with less opportunity for error.

This additional information includes:

- Status (gauge active and in use, or removed from service, or out for repair)
- Location (the physical location or employee who possesses it)
- The person responsible for gauge's calibration
- Gauge units of measure and functional range
- The standard name and number to be used
- The points on the gauge that are to be checked
- The checkpoint tolerances and result rounding rules
- Description, type, and class, if applicable
- Manufacturer
- Criteria for visual inspection for damage
- Criteria for fitness for use (visual examination only; no measurements taken)
- Photographs of equipment to aid in identification

This additional information gives us guidance for how each calibration is to be performed and further identifies the individual gauge.

■ ■ ■

Even with all this extra data, the system thus far is still only a recall system. It is a *reference* tool. It merely allows gauges to be retrieved and calibrated, on time, per a given procedure.

MOVING BEYOND THE SIMPLE RECALL SYSTEM

To have a fully complete calibration system we must build upon the core recall system. We should include a means to enter and manage the data resulting from the calibrations. We must create historical records for each calibration event in order to show proof of our actions. Whereas a paper trail of worksheets printed from your recall system and filled in by technicians can meet the requirement of proof, it is not considered the best practice due to the many frailties of paper. Paper can be lost or destroyed and is hard to search even with the best filing system. If you must use paper without data entry into your database, consider scanning all completed documents into an electronic format. Scanning and electronic filing offers better protection against loss or damage and makes searching somewhat easier.

The best system, however, requires the entry of data for each calibration event into the database. In addition to all the information from the recall system mentioned earlier, we also capture the actual measurement data for each checkpoint. We see the variance from each checkpoint and if the measurement is in tolerance. If fit-for-use inspection is required instead of checkpoints, we can log the results of such inspections. We create a permanent database record, easily searched, of what actions were taken and by whom, and whether the gauge was adjusted or repaired.

OUT-OF-TOLERANCE CONDITIONS

Remember that the goal of a complete calibration system is to ensure all the gauges and instruments we use for processing and testing are giving us accurate results. What do we do when we find a gauge out of tolerance? This situation will occur and we must have protocols in place to handle such issues. The protocols you create for this situation depend on your knowledge of the process, the meaningfulness of the measurement, and the acceptable level of risk. Here are some guidelines to help you develop your own plan of action given no other guidance by specification or regulation.

First, determine how critical the measurement is to product quality and the severity of the out-of-tolerance condition. For example, the measurement could be for process control only—checks that are taken only to ensure the equipment is running efficiently and is cost effective. In this case, the only action required is to repair or replace the gauge since the measurement truly did not affect the product quality or function. The only loss here is an internal one.

Measurements for quality control, compliance to specifications, and certifications require a different protocol. All material produced and tested with the defective gauge, and thought compliant, must not be allowed to proceed to customers, or the next step in processing, until the suspected measurement can be verified by a known good instrument. Steps must be taken to quarantine all suspect materials and remove them from the production stream. This protocol is exactly the same as for failed testing. *All* product made since the last known good calibration for that gauge must be identified, quarantined, and verified. The scale of this can be very large. The quarantined material should be checked again with a gauge that is in tolerance, and testing of quarantined material should follow a more tightened sampling plan than normal. If suspect material is found to be compliant, it may be released back into production or allowed to ship. If found to be noncompliant, product must remain in quarantine and disposition made based on your established procedures for nonconforming materials.

If the situation is such that material checked with an inaccurate gauge is already in the next process or, worse, in the field, you must be prepared to notify all potentially affected customers of the error and plan for recalling, replacing, or repairing the suspect product.

In every out-of-tolerance situation, a record of every aspect of the quarantine, and all steps taken such as retesting, tightened sampling plan, and release authority, must be captured and documented along with the calibration data for the defective gauge. We desire to create a link between that gauge and product, and show evidence of all our actions to verify the product, the results of that evaluation, and its final disposition.

The potential impact to your production operations and business profits is huge when critical gauges are found to be inaccurate. In high-capacity operations, a large amount of product can be affected by a bad gauge when calibration frequencies are set far apart. It is a better practice to calibrate more often until assurance can be had that the gauge is stable and accurate. Only then can you consider lengthening the period between calibrations. So as you design your calibration system, take the time to really think through the protocols for calibration and calibration frequencies. Remember every gauge is considered guilty until proven innocent. Create your out-of-tolerance plan in advance and treat it as you would a disaster plan. Everyone needs to know what to do to minimize the damage when, not if, a gauge fails.

FINAL THOUGHTS

As you read this book, you may find yourself questioning the effort and expense required to implement some of the systems discussed. In this case, having a calibration system *is not debatable*. You must be able to gauge the attributes of the items you manufacture with *absolute confidence*. The quality of your product is only as good as your ability to measure its properties. A well-planned, -executed, and -managed calibration system creates this solid foundation of validity for all your testing and verification measurements. Upon this foundation you may place your confidence that your product actually meets requirements, as well as the assurance that you are delivering a product that meets the expectations of your customers.

CHAPTER 5

Corrective and Preventative Action and Error Proofing

It was in May 1996 that ValuJet flight 592 crashed into the Everglades of Florida, killing everyone aboard. Investigation revealed the crash was caused by oxygen generation canisters being transported in the cargo hold. It was determined that one of these canisters accidentally activated during the plane's taxi. These canisters were improperly prepared for transport and were in fact not permitted by law to be transported in the cargo hold. These canisters create oxygen through a chemical reaction that creates heat as a byproduct. The combination of heat and oxygen was enough to create and sustain the fatal fire that bypassed the plane's fire suppression systems.

Corrective action was taken after the investigation and new laws enacted to govern the transportation of oxygen canisters. The regulation, Department of Transportation's Pipeline and Hazardous Materials Safety Administration (PHMSA) Rule HM-224B (CFR 49 Parts 173, 175, and 178) requires all such canisters be transported in cases specially designed to prevent the canisters from becoming involved in a fire.

The regulation calls out for all such cases to pass a flame-penetration test in which the case must withstand a 1,700°F flame for five minutes. Additionally, the temperature four inches above the canister inside the case must not exceed 400°F. Finally, the case must pass a *thermal resistance test* in which the case is baked in an oven at 400°F for three hours. The temperature of the canister must not exceed 199°F.

Air transportation is well known for taking corrective action to prevent future accidents. In manufacturing we are daily called upon to do the very same thing. While we may not be faced with such extreme situations as a plane crash, we are charged with investigation and resolution of issues when we miss the mark on quality or performance.

Most companies, even very large ones, drop the ball occasionally. Every company has a customer complaint department, or should. Every company also has internal issues where some process or procedure failed. Therefore, we must have a way to collect, manage, and resolve these issues and ensure they do not occur again.

In all my years of being involved in quality control, nothing strikes more fear in the hearts of management and staff than the term *corrective action*. Some managers feel receiving a corrective action is a negative reflection on their ability to manage. Nothing is further from the truth. Corrective action requests are opportunities to make improvements. Willingness to improve is the hallmark of a good manager. Manufacturers who embrace best practices know you cannot have the very *best* practices without making mistakes along the way. It is how we learn. So in our suite of tools we must include a system that helps us manage these opportunities when they arise. A corrective action system, like the other systems we have covered, is another way to document our recognition of an issue and the steps we took to address it. Your customers look far more favorably on you when there is real solid evidence that efforts are being made to correct a problem. Corrective action is the fire that refines everything we do.

To make corrective action a best practice we need to forge a system and some rules for its use. We also need to arm ourselves with tools that help us with the investigation process and resolution. This system, just like all the others, is multifaceted. So let's look at each piece in turn and how it supports all the others.

First, I want to clarify the term. Corrective action is *not* a punishment tool or disciplinary action. I have seen systems used in this manner and this attitude misses the point entirely. The misuse of the system in this way is the very reason so many managers despise receiving a corrective action request. It recalls negative feelings of bad grades in school. So, from the very beginning, we need to educate our fellow managers that the purpose of a corrective action is to help us track down where we, as management, failed to provide adequate procedures to prevent an error and then work together to find an agreed solution. Receipt of a corrective action is not a personal commentary on someone's ability, neither is it a personal attack.

WHEN IS CORRECTIVE ACTION REQUIRED?

Sometimes the most challenging problem is the decision on when a corrective action is needed. You can literally drown yourself and the organization with corrective actions if one is issued for each minor error or mistake someone makes. People make mistakes, that is a given, and a corrective action system that is overused leads to the aforementioned fear most people have of this system. Minor day-to-day problems should be handled as they occur, using nothing more than good management practices.

As I see it, corrective action is required in two instances: first, when seemingly minor problems become chronic, and second, when there is an obvious flaw in any system that allows costly errors to be made and adversely affect product quality or employee safety. The corrective action system we design must be able to handle these instances internally within our organization. In addition, our system must extend to cover issues with our suppliers of goods and services and be able to manage incoming requests for corrective action from our external customers.

As I said before, daily mistakes are expected and normal as long as we have people doing jobs. However, as in the first scenario, when we see the same mistake occurring on a regular basis, this points to a deeper cause. There is obviously a problem with the instructions or process. The procedures may be incomplete, unclear, or missing altogether. The process may not be well documented. Rarely, if ever, is it an employee trying to do a bad job. Most likely, the cause is an internal system breakdown.

In the second scenario, the decision for corrective action is glaringly obvious. A missing quality check allows your product to ship out of specification. A major product failure in the field prompts a return or recall. A supplier ships you incorrect or mislabeled raw material. A procedure puts your employee in a dangerous situation. Many times your external customer will require written corrective action for quality issues as a part of doing business with you. All these are real-life examples that have a real impact on our profitability, people, and customers. Situations like these must be corrected and our actions documented to serve as evidence. As with our product testing system, our corrective action system must leave no doubt or loose ends regarding the problem, our investigation, and our steps for remediation.

REQUIREMENTS FOR A CORRECTIVE ACTION SYSTEM

Like other systems we've discussed, the corrective action system has key data elements it must contain. This system, as with others, may be manual or computerized. The computerized system is the practice of choice here due to the large amount of data and requirements for tracking follow-up actions. You may develop your system internally or purchase one of the many fine software titles available. No matter your preference, the following data elements should be included:

- A unique incident identification number
- Date of request
- Corrective action status (active or completed)
- Name of person making request and title
- Request source (internal, customer, supplier) and contact information
- External request identification number, if applicable
- External part number
- Complete description of the problem, including pictures and any supporting documentation
- What product is involved, the quantity, lot number, or any other identifying data
- What functional area is responsible for the error, if known
- Who in your organization entered the corrective action and date
- Person responsible for the investigation
- Who has been assigned action items for the investigation (may be different from overall responsibility)
- Person responsible for the resolution, the actions required, and action due date
- Actions taken to contain any defective material, if applicable

- Results of root cause investigation
- Complete report of all actions taken to identify and correct root cause, including details of all process changes made, document updates, employee counseling, and dates for each
- Final response date
- Due date for corrective action effectiveness follow-up and person responsible
- Copies of all documentation that was sent to internal/external sources

Unless otherwise noted, each data element should contain information for each incident. This list of data elements creates an outline to guide you through the steps in your investigation and ensures consistency. Depending on the sophistication of your system, you may create automated prompts to notify users of missing information, due or overdue issues, and follow-up actions. A computerized system should also have provisions to easily retrieve issues based on due dates.

■ ■ ■

Now that we have a means to manage the data for a corrective action, how do we go about conducting an investigation?

INVESTIGATING AND RESOLVING A CORRECTIVE ACTION ISSUE

As mentioned previously, corrective action is required because something went wrong in a process or procedure that created an undesirable situation or product problem. The goal here is to determine what is known as the *root cause*. Root cause is the original condition that leads to the eventual failure. The root cause may be found to occur at any point in your processing. Root cause may not always be obvious. Events or situations that appear totally unrelated to the manifested problem can be the genesis of the issue. We must therefore work backward from the problem condition through each process step until we reach a probable cause and its associated process.

The first step of investigation is to clearly define the problem in exacting detail. The better defined the issue, the more clearly focused the investigation and the less time spent chasing unrelated details. So when the problem first arises, gather as much detail as possible from your complaint source while the issue is still fresh. This speeds along the investigation steps and can sometimes point directly to the root cause itself without a lot of additional effort. As we shall see in the next example, the clarity with which the problem is defined is the compass that steers the investigation.

For example, here are four ways a customer could describe the same issue:

1. Customer states that item does not work.
2. Customer states that item appears damaged.
3. Customer states that carton containing item was crushed.
4. Customer states that carton containing item was crushed when delivered by your new trucking company.

Clearly, these four citations could be very different problems warranting different investigation paths:

In the first example, *item does not work*, you could be inclined to look to internal processes, quality control checks, and testing to see how a defective product was allowed to ship.

In the second example, *item appears damaged*, your focus then moves from production problems to perhaps final inspection or your warehousing and material handling areas.

In the third example, *carton crushed* could indicate a problem with your packaging area or carton vendor.

In the final example, *carton crushed by new delivery company*, you look to the new outside delivery vendor as the source of the problem. A carton crushed by the new delivery company certainly can damage the item and, if so, the damaged item will not work properly.

So we see that both the initial definition of the issue and the subsequent root cause analysis can utilize the same investigative techniques. Expecting that we may be getting only part of the story, we need a method that both guides our questioning and allows us to step backward through our process to find a probable cause. Once found, we can investigate further to determine whether the probable cause is indeed the root cause.

There are many good techniques for this brainstorming exercise, but I prefer a simple process of asking *why* as many times as needed until I can go no further or until I hit a likely probable cause. Much like when a child incessantly asks *why* to every answer you give, you will eventually run out of answers. In manufacturing, this end point most likely occurs at the root cause, or very close to it.

Returning to our example citations, it is clear that the answer to the question *why* can lead to the next level of detail. Let's use this technique to work through our example:

Item does not work.

Why?

Item was damaged.

Why?

Carton was crushed.

Why?

Carton delivered by new trucking company.

Is this our final answer, or can we ask why again? Let's see:

Carton was delivered by new trucking company.

Why?

New trucking company was chosen because of cheaper rates than the old trucker and it offered same service.

Why?

Cost-cutting measure.

Why?

Decreased cost equals increased profitability.

Why?

Company wants to be profitable, and so on.

So it's clear from this line of questioning that the decision to simply replace the trucking company based solely on cost is the probable cause. But we must then ask ourselves once more, *why?* What went wrong with our decision process to replace a trucking company and how did that decision cause the issue?

Further investigation of our probable cause shows we have no internal requirements to evaluate and approve new vendors. There are no procedures for audits or scorecards. There was no requirement to interview the vendor's current clients to see if our new trucking candidate has issues with damaged deliveries. So our practice of choosing an outside vendor based *solely on cost alone* and without regard for the ability to perform is the true root cause of our current complaint.

You may wish to take a moment and read through this section again to solidify the idea that the complaint and the root cause, viewed together, appear totally unrelated. Yet through the process of asking *why*, and stepping backward, you can establish a link. As I mentioned in the beginning, if you have the opportunity to use this technique when taking the initial complaint, you can save a great deal of time in the research process and respond more quickly to your customer.

CORRECTIVE ACTION RESOLUTION

Discovering the root cause is only half the battle. We must now address what actions to take to correct and, more importantly, prevent the same problem from occurring again. Corrective actions must be well thought out, enforceable, and, most importantly, have the ability to be *audited*.

In designing and thinking through our corrective action, we have to test our ideas for loopholes and weaknesses that could allow for the same mistakes to reoccur. If the proposed actions to be taken involve many people, or cross departments, it is best to have more than one person evaluate the actions. There may be knowledge possessed by individuals of which we are not aware, that may have bearing on the actions required to address the deficiency. Once you are reasonably sure of your action plan, it is best to try it out with the *why* process once again to test for any weaknesses.

One of the key elements to any good corrective action is the ability to be audited. Corrective actions will involve a procedural change and necessitate the update, or creation, of documents to capture the new information. These documents become the reference material for the audit. The updated documents must be covered with all affected employees as required in your document control and training plans. It is a good practice to include a complete explanation of the original error in all document updates. The explanation is usually captured in the revision history log for the document and serves as a reference for anyone who may question why the procedural changes are necessary. Changes in established procedures or the creation of new procedures are the most vulnerable for mistakes during the early days of implementation. We must therefore conduct the first audit immediately after the corrective action is fully in force to ensure the new procedures are being understood and followed; otherwise, the original error can happen again.

Depending on the severity of the original error, subsequent follow-up audits should be undertaken frequently until all the audit findings show no evidence of recurrence. Only then can you consider the problem resolved and the corrective action incident closed. Document all audit results and evidence for closure in your corrective action system.

ERROR PROOFING

Best practices for corrective action would not be complete without a discussion on error proofing. Error proofing is a design method that can be used at any time but is especially useful during resolution planning for a corrective action. Error proofing is best described as actions taken to *absolutely guarantee* the problem issue cannot happen again and typically involves more than simple written procedural changes. Here are three examples of problems and suggested error-proofing measures.

This first example is one we can all relate to: the lost gas cap. When filling our car with gas, we must remove the gas cap to access the tank. Typically, the gas cap is completely removable and must be either held in the hand or placed somewhere, like on top of the gas pump or car roof, while we fill the tank. The unattached cap can be forgotten and left behind, or lost as we drive away. Error proofing in this case is as simple as having a cable that attaches the cap to the car and prevents the physical separation. While we may still drive away forgetting to replace the cap, it is nonetheless still dangling there, attached to the car, when we discover our error.

Our second example concerns safety. Safety is always a priority in manufacturing. Having an employee injured on the job is the type of error that must be prevented at all costs. Our safety programs are a great place to see error proofing in action and are useful in helping us develop the thought process for new error-proofing ideas.

A die stamp press is a useful example here. Most die stamps consist of a die or form attached to either a very heavy weight or hydraulic press. These stamps exert tons of force to form metal into parts and strike very quickly. The loading and unloading of the press is often done manually, requiring the employee's hands to reach inside the working area of the press. The obvious error we must prevent is employee injury.

The press is equipped with two start buttons that must be activated at the same time and are placed far enough apart to require the use of both hands by the operator. This ensures the operator's hands are clear of the striking surfaces. This, however, is not enough. The two start buttons are no guarantee of safety to another employee in the area. Therefore, the press is also surrounded by a wire mesh cage with a single sliding panel as the only means of entry. The panel is located directly in front of the operator and is connected into the electrical controls of the press. The machine's two start buttons cannot engage while the cage door is open and the press area exposed.

While these physical measures error-proof the possibility of hand injury, they are still not complete. Since we are using physical devices like switches and cages to accomplish our error-proofing plan, we must not forget that physical devices can sometimes fail as well. Maintenance and inspection of all the safety equipment on the machine must be done on a regular basis. I recommend that operators test all safety measures at the start of each shift as part of their daily routine and the equipment be given complete maintenance on a scheduled frequency.

Our final scenario does not make use of a hardware deterrent to error, but rather software. With the use of computers so ingrained in our businesses today, and so much data being entered by people into these systems, errors are common. A simple example is entering a customer's mailing address. One of the vital pieces of information we must have is the Zip Code. A missing or invalid Zip Code may cause our mail to be rejected or misdirected. Communication delays like these can have a serious impact on both our customers and ourselves. Error proofing this situation requires programming the computer system to require entry of the Zip Code. Failure to do so gives an error message to the operator and prevents the operator from proceeding until the required data is provided.

Simply requiring data to be present, however, is only the first step in error proofing this process. Just because we enter data for the Zip Code does not make that data valid, *only present*. Our system programming must also include a validation step that compares the data entered against a database of valid Zip Codes. If the data entered is found in the database, we are assured the Zip Code is valid. If not found, we once again do not allow updates and prevent moving to the next step. With both these edits in place, we are assured of capturing the correct information we need.

These three examples should make it clear that error proofing helps secure your corrective action plan by halting the work flow if requirements are not met. So, when you need to formulate a corrective action for an issue, it is best practice to include error proofing in your action plan.

■ ■ ■

As I stated in the beginning of this chapter, managers sometimes have difficulty with the idea of corrective action. I have shown how properly researched and implemented corrective action, along with error proofing, can actually make managers' duties easier by preventing errors. Every error prevented decreases the effort spent in fire-fighting and returns valuable time to the manager for more valuable tasks such as process and quality improvements.

PREVENTATIVE ACTION

From a quality point of view, corrective action is a reactive process. The problem has already occurred and we must *react* to it. The absolute best corrective action is the one you never have to take. Preventative action addresses this idea. Preventative action is proactive; it seeks to identify potential problems before they happen and establish an action plan to prevent their occurrence.

Documentation of preventative actions attests to your commitment to quality improvements. Much, but not all, of the data required to create a preventative action plan is the same as that required for corrective action. Preventative actions may be easily incorporated into the same corrective action tracking system you already have in place simply by adding another classification category to flag these entries.

The processes of brainstorming and resolution for preventative actions are essentially the same as for corrective actions. Preventative action embraces the principles of error proofing as well. The difference is in what triggers the request. Preventative action requests have multiple sources. Among these are employee suggestions or concerns, findings from an internal audit, or feedback from formalized process improvement teams. To reiterate, preventative action seeks to identify potential problems before they occur and create a plan to prevent occurrence in the first place. Corrective action and error proofing address situations that have already occurred and work to prevent recurrence.

An example should help clarify the difference.

An internal team is conducting an audit of work instructions in a parts fabrication department. The audit is routine and the audit's purpose is the verification that instructions are being followed as written and match current practices being utilized on the shop floor.

One particular instruction being audited has the requirement to attach process paperwork to the outside of a container of parts. This paperwork authorizes the release of the batch to the next manufacturing department and contains information that is used in the setup of the equipment in the next process. This setup information is batch-number-specific, and must be clearly written and attached to the correct container. The placement of the paperwork on the outside of the container is also a visual clue to the next department that the container is ready for subsequent processing.

During the audit a couple of observations were made. These observations, while not directly within the scope of the current work instruction or audit, are nonetheless noteworthy and were included in the team findings.

First, there were containers of parts that appeared complete but did not have paperwork attached to the outside. Upon closer examination the paperwork was found to have accidentally fallen inside the container. Discussion with the operator revealed this happens frequently because the production area is very humid and the paperwork is simply attached to the container with a piece of masking tape. The operator also explained that sometimes the paperwork gets lost entirely, which then requires extensive research to assure the identity of the batch, recreate the documentation, and reunite the documents with the container.

Second, this finding led the audit team to look at several other containers. While most had the paperwork attached on the outside and in plain sight, the information written on sheets was smudged or illegible. The sheets were filled out by operators either with pencil or pen. Subsequent handling or simply being exposed to the humid environment caused the writing to become damaged.

Whereas to date these situations have not caused any major problems other than frustration, we can identify at least three potential issues stemming from these observations:

1. Containers missing the visual clue of paperwork on the outside of the container will be ignored as ready for the next process step. Until someone investigates and attaches the paperwork, processing and delivery is delayed.

2. Containers separated from their paperwork become orphaned and require great effort to correctly identify and assure the next process is set up correctly.

3. Damaged or illegible information on the sheets may cause an incorrect setup of the next process, resulting in quality issues, rework, or waste.

While *all three* theoretical problems may never happen, the potential fallout from any single occurrence can have serious consequences.

Our audit team found no noncompliance regarding the work instruction; everyone was following the instructions exactly as written. Therefore, no corrective action was required. However, based on the observations, it was clear that preventative measures were needed. The audit observations were recorded as suggested preventative actions in our database and assignments made to department managers. The response actions taken were both physical and procedural.

The first measure was to ensure the work documents were present, visible, and protected. The masking tape method was replaced by the following: All containers in the department were outfitted with clear, rigid plastic sleeves. These sleeves were permanently attached to the containers by rivets, located in the same spot on each container, and clearly marked PAPERWORK.

Next, work procedures were updated to include instructions about the use of the new sleeves, specifically prohibited any other method, and required all containers be staged so the sleeves were clearly visible to material handlers.

Finally, procedures now require all paperwork be written out with indelible markers to prevent smudging and all workstations be supplied with approved markers.

Our example clearly illustrates how observing what is happening around you and taking action before an issue occurs can lead to optimized productivity and minimized losses.

FINAL THOUGHTS

I hope it is now clear to you that the use of a formalized corrective action system is not a negative thing but is in fact a tremendous asset in your plan to improve product quality and processes. Truthfully, I do not believe you can be successful in manufacturing without such a system. Through use of the investigative techniques I've outlined, this system can *guarantee successful investigation and resolution* of any issue that arises. Coupled with error proofing and preventative action, you build a solid quality system core that creates product consistency, lowers production cost, and, most importantly, gives your customers an exceptional product experience.

CHAPTER 6

Document Control: Ensuring Vital Information Is Available to Those Who Need It

The Universal Widget Company (UWC) produces plastic widgets used around the world as component parts in everything from automobiles to appliances. Recently, during an internal review, UWC discovered a quality issue with one of its new products. The inquiry revealed a miscalculation on the formula for the plastic mix. With the root cause being found, the engineering team revised the plastic formula and the UWC team considered the problem fixed.

Then the phone calls and e-mails started pouring in from around the world. Widgets were failing in the field in large numbers. UWC initiated a widget recall that cost millions of dollars and damaged its reputation in the industry. Needless to say, an investigation was launched.

"How can this be?" the engineers thought. "We updated the formula!" This was indeed true—they did. UWC's true failure was not so much in the product itself but in the area of document control.

Investigation revealed that the formula document contains no identification other than its title. The formula has no revision control or accountability. It is impossible to tell between two versions of the document which is the latest. Also, the formula document was not an accountable form. This means there is no way to know how many copies of this formula exist or where they are located.

Investigation findings show that the formula document currently in use on the shop floor was the prior version and was kept in a notebook by the operator along with some handwritten notes. Implementation cost of a document control system for UWC would have been very small compared to the cost of the recall and lost business.

If information is the lifeblood of manufacturing, then undoubtedly, documents, in all their forms, are the veins through which it flows. It is clear, then, that in our quest for best practices, we must address how to control this stream of information.

WHY GO TO ALL THIS EFFORT?

I think that from the opening horror story the answer to this question is obvious. For every step of the manufacturing process, there must be clearly defined instructions, procedures, and requirements in order to create a product that meets your customer's expectations for quality, features, price, and function. Somehow, we must be able to disseminate this information and deliver it into the hands of those who need it.

A typical manufacturing environment, for example, uses some sort of journal, shop order, or batch sheet that follows the product through all the subsequent steps of production. These documents not only identify the physical item but may also contain references to instructions for the work to be performed or a quality inspection point. These shop orders should reference not only the instruction name but also its revision number. We can be reasonably sure that our product will be produced/tested with the correct and most recently approved methods by matching the shop order instruction back to the actual document, by its title and revision. Working from a common set of documents also betters our chances of everyone performing the same job in the same way.

One important note to remember here: We must not only train our employees to perform this revision verification but also empower them to cease any further work in the event of mismatched information. Another vital piece to document control is banning all personal notes, cheat sheets, or other sources of information. We should encourage our employees to openly share any information they may have about a particular process in order to capture that knowledge in the official document.

It's easy to see that document control gives us an effective method to ensure we have the latest complete information available on the shop floor. How do we accomplish this?

Long gone are the days when the sole means of document distribution was the printed page. In today's modern manufacturing environment, documentation comes in myriad forms such as web pages, CAD drawings, PDF attachments, or control files for computer-controlled machines, to name a few. Yet, in spite of all the technological advancements available, most companies usually utilize some of these new techniques blended with the more traditional printed page. These documentation methods can be grouped into two families: printed and electronic.

Both of these documentation methods can be found in most manufacturing environments today. That being true, the best practices in documentation control center around how to ensure delivery or accessibility of the *latest* information. How do we prevent outdated information from reaching the shop floor?

PAPER-BASED SYSTEMS

When working with a printed document we have to understand that the information on that document is potentially dead the moment it leaves the printer. We have *set in stone* the information contained on it. If the information we hold in our hands suddenly changes, how are we to know? How can we be sure the document is complete and that we truly have a complete set of instructions?

Best practice dictates we address four elements: first, a means to identify our document as the most current; second, a way to verify we possess the document in its entirety; third, a method to match the document to the known requirements from our customers or manufacturing methods and standards; and finally, a system of document management that consists of document distribution and retrieval and that makes available only the latest versions of the documents.

■ ■ ■

The answer to all these elements we shall call *revision control and document distribution*.

REVISION CONTROL

The best and most simple method of revision control is by means of the *document control box*. Simple in its nature, each document we generate should contain the following minimum information:

- Unique document name
- Revision level or sequence
- Revision date
- Revision replaced
- Revision replaced date
- Page numbering with total pages
- Authorization of the document by signature/title

See Figure 6.1 for a two-page excerpt from a five-page work instruction. The revision control block is in the upper right-hand corner of each page.

Each page of the document must contain all the information shown, except for the authorization. The authorization signature can be only on page 1 and is sufficient as long as each of the subsequent pages contains the rest of the control block.

As you can see, use of the document control box gives us: (1) an easy way to quickly see we have the complete document via page numbering; (2) a reference point for which revision level we need to be working from and its age; and (3) an authorizing agent or contact for any questions that may arise.

DOCUMENT DISTRIBUTION

Now that we have all our paper documents properly identified and authorized, we need a way of organizing the documents into manageable groups. We must also control the number of copies in circulation, implement a retrieval/replacement system for keeping documents updated, and create a means for identifying counterfeit or illegal copies of documents while providing a legal method for uncontrolled copies outside our system.

We manage our documents by grouping like documents together to create procedures manuals. These manuals then contain an index

Procedure: How to Mow the Lawn
Revision 3 Dated: 05/13/2009
Replaces Revision 2 Dated: 01/01/2009
Page 1 of 5
Authorized by: *Joe Bermuda* / Senior Landscaper

This procedure covers the use of gasoline-powered lawn equipment for cutting grass surfaces to the required lengths.

Before beginning the mowing session, gather all required equipment and be sure to have read and understood each section of this procedure. If there are any missing or defective equipment, safety concerns, or questions, see your supervisor before proceeding.

Equipment Required:

1. Gasoline-powered grass mower with minimum 36-inch cut.

2. 1 gallon red approved safety gasoline can filled with 87 octane gasoline.

3. Eye protection—full goggles recommended.

4. Hearing protection—ear plugs minimum—full ear muffs recommended.

5. Long-sleeved shirt and long pants.

6. Leather shoes that cover the ankle with treaded bottoms—steel toes recommended.

7. Gloves that do not restrict hand movement.

Safety Check

Before performing any safety check on the mower, disconnect the wire from the spark plug and be sure the starter switch is in the ***off*** position.

Visually inspect the blade for condition issues such as chips, cracks, or breaks. If blade is deemed unsafe, see ***Blade Replacement Procedure***.

Remove any dried grass that may block exits using a gloved hand or by washing with hose.

Examine rest of mower for any damage that may affect safe operation.

When safety check is completed, reattach wire to spark plug and proceed to the ***Fueling***.

Figure 6.1 Excerpt from a Work Instruction

Procedure: How to Mow the Lawn
Revision 3 Dated: 05/13/2009
Replaces Revision 2 Dated: 01/01/2009
Page 2 of 5

Fueling

Gasoline is an extremely volatile and toxic fuel and must be handled with care. No smoking is allowed within 100 feet of any equipment being fueled. Eating and drinking while fueling any equipment is expressly prohibited.

Equipment may contain residual fuel, causing pressure in the tank. Remove the mower's fuel cap by rotating slowly clockwise and listen for any sound of escaping pressure. Allow all pressure to vent before removing cap completely.

With the cap removed, fill the tank to within one inch from the top with gasoline from the red can. If overrun or spillage occurs, see ***Clean UP Procedure*** section.

Preexisting Conditions

Before starting to mow, walk around the entire area to be mowed looking for any loose debris or obstacles that may become a hazard while mowing. Remove and discard any items found.

AND SO ON . . .

Figure 6.1 *(Continued)*

page showing the list of documents contained within and each document's current revision level. This index, itself, has its own revision control block to ensure that it, too, is the most current. There shall be one, and only one, master copy of each manual, which is usually held by the manual's owner.

Finally, at the topmost level of document control resides the master list of all manuals, which, as you can guess by now, has an index of the manuals, their most current revision, how many copies of the manual exist, and who is in possession of them. Taken together, all this constitutes a family tree of our documentation, giving us reference points as to what is current.

Controlling the number of documents in circulation is as easy as designating each set of documents and manuals with a number. For example, if there are five copies of a manual, then each page in that manual is stamped with its own unique corresponding number. This stamp is usually colored so that if the page is copied on a typical black/white copier, the number renders black. This provides an easy method of monitoring for uncontrolled copies. I will go more into depth on uncontrolled documents later.

A system of documentation that is alive and working will generally have frequent updates. Affected documents will need to be updated as new and better methods become available, clarification of current instructions are found, or process changes occur. Therefore, someone needs to be the caretaker responsible for making fresh documents available. All documents and manuals, therefore, should have a single owner. The owner may be an individual or may be an entire department like Quality Assurance. The owner is responsible for all documentation updates and tasked with the duty of distribution of new/ updated documents.

A critical piece of document control is the verification that all old copies of a procedure are replaced when a new copy is issued. This is where having an index and numbered manuals can assist us. After a new update is issued, the subsequently returned copies are checked off one by one against the old index for the master manual. Each returned copy is noted on the index with its return date. A quick scan of the old index provides us with a quick audit of who has or has not returned a replaced document. Once all documents are returned, we can simply file the old master index, along with the notations of when copies were returned, and include the master copy of the old procedure. This package gives us a completely traceable record of this update transaction.

UNCONTROLLED COPIES

Sometimes, it may be necessary to have a copy of a controlled document outside our control system. Requests from customers, meeting reference material, or an offsite job may require us to have a copy of some document in hand. In cases like these, we have to be certain the person holding the document is well aware that the information he holds is outside our controlled environment. It is wise, therefore, to have some method to identify these documents. A simple rubber stamp with the words UNCONTROLLED COPY is sufficient. Stamp each and every page before turning it over to your requester. There are also special printing papers available for your controlled copies that contain UNCONTROLLED COPY in a fine microprint that is not visible on the original but is revealed when exposed in a photocopier. Although this method is a more expensive alternative, it does remove the need for human intervention to stamp or mark the copied material.

Use of the UNCONTROLLED mark accomplishes a couple of objectives. First, it makes it clear to the document holder that he may or may not hold the most recent copy, and will not be receiving any updates. Second, it allows for easy auditing for legitimacy of any loose instructions found floating around on the shop floor.

ELECTRONICALLY BASED SYSTEMS

Today, more than ever before, companies are moving away from paper-driven systems where practical. The use of electronic (web-based) sources for information is becoming commonplace. This move greatly facilitates document control. Web-based documents require far less human intervention for maintenance and distribution. This is not to say the control measures required by a paper system are no longer necessary. We still need control measures to ensure we are making the latest information available to our production areas.

Web-based systems offer the following advantages due to the fact that the information is universally available as soon as it is published by the document owner:

- Physical signoff of documents is eliminated since the authorizing agent is usually the one publishing the document.
- There is no need for multiple copies of either documents or manuals. Information is globally available.
- Without physical manuals and documents we also eliminate the need for unique numbering of manuals.
- The check-off process for manual/procedure updates is eliminated since old information is removed as soon as the website is updated.
- Indexes are no longer really necessary, but may be retained in the web-based system as an organizational tool.

Web-based documents should retain, however, some form of the document control block. Even with web-based documentation we must still provide some means to match the published information to any requirements in production areas.

The management of documents by electronic means is truly an elegant best practice solution to the control problem.

GUIDELINES AND AUDITS

No discussion about best practices would be complete without touching on setting up guidelines and audit protocols to ensure our system accomplishes what we designed it to do.

The following points are absolute musts:

- No handwritten notes, notebooks, sticky notes, or personal documents are to be used in any area. Handwritten notes are one individual's version of the truth and most likely will not contain complete or current information. Finding lots of personal notes on your shop floor is a sure sign that the instructions your documentation system is providing are incomplete, hard to access, or not understandable.

- If you are using a web-based system, you should not allow printouts of web pages to be used, unless printing a document from the Web is addressed and managed by the control measures set up for paper documents.

- Periodic audits of the shop floor are necessary to find weaknesses in the system. A simple walk through production areas with a master manual in hand and matching distributed documents to the master index is a quick verification step. Being observant of any paper documents lying around the workplace will often reveal illegal notes. Asking employees to describe how they perform their duties will sometimes yield hidden notes and documents.

Please understand that this is not a witch hunt. In cases where audits uncover illegal documentation, we must reassure the employees that we want merely to understand why they need the information, and seek out ways to improve our system to include it. Constant monitoring of our documentation and its control systems ensures our methods become best practices.

FINAL THOUGHTS

I think you can now see that information and the control of information are vital to any manufacturing endeavor.

Utilizing the best practices approach to document control is a cornerstone of achieving our goal to produce a quality product, on time, at the right price, and with the right features.

In summary, document control best practices include the following:

- Revision control of documents and indexes give quick reference to ensure most recent information is used.
- Distribution control keeps outdated information off the shop floor.
- Electronic distribution is the best method because it creates a single repository of data, thus eliminating all of the problems of revision and retrieval.
- Handwritten personal notes, while not allowed, give insight into the weaknesses of our current control system and offer opportunities to improve.

CHAPTER **7**

Process Control

The Fast Press Printing Company is a small bulk printer specializing in short production runs. A typical press run for them would yield a final roll of product no more than 5,000 meters in length. The majority of their clients are bulk mail advertisers and as such the printing is usually done on very cheap recycled rag paper. Equipment setup is pretty much the same for every run. The key product characteristics are good alignment of the four-color print and a good build of the final roll. The roll build is critical to the next step in the process, which is cutting. The printed roll needs to be built with smooth sides that are perpendicular to its core. This build allows the paper to be aligned evenly to feed into the precision cutting equipment in the next process.

Fast Press recently received a new client and a lesson in process control. The new client requested the printing to be done on a coated paper whose surface was very slick and shiny like that used for magazines. Printing on this different type of paper was a new challenge for Fast Press. With order in hand, the press operators began the equipment setup as usual. Toward the end of the first roll things started to take a turn for the worse in a big way.

The massive roll started to wind unevenly. The top-third of the roll began to shift to one side. Rather than having smooth sides, it was becoming cone-shaped. The longer the roll ran, the more like an ice cream cone it appeared. This misalignment subsequently affected the registration of the colors and the print quality. Production was quickly halted and the first roll was ruined.

Investigation revealed that a key process variable called "winding tension" was not addressed. Winding tension is the amount of force, or pull, applied to the paper as it is wound to allow it to roll up properly on the center core. Before, the operators were used to only one type of paper so there was never a need to consider any adjustment to tension. Due to the new paper's smoother surface, the tension settings were too high. This resulted in too much force being applied as the roll grew. Finally, the tension overcame the internal frictional forces holding the roll in alignment and the roll slipped.

This example illustrates the need to understand that every process has its unique set of key variables that are required to produce our products. Given this understanding we must then set about to define those key variables. The example also points out the need to have a process control plan to guide us in establishing equipment setup, process monitoring, and machine capabilities.

How do you design and implement a process to produce a product that meets customer demands? Process control is a set of methods and procedures that, if implemented correctly, take much of the guesswork out of manufacturing products to meet customer needs. Process control measures also help to reduce waste and scrap rates, improve first-pass yields, minimize rework, and reduce the possibility of field failures and returns. In reality, process control allows you to build quality into your product through a strict system of checks and balances instead of trial and error, guesswork, or opinion. Only artists create products based on a touchy-feely, pleasing-to-the-eye set of standards. Consistently manufacturing quality products requires a disciplined approach. Having a robust process control plan helps you accomplish that goal.

One can never have enough control measures in place in any process. The more control you have in your manufacturing environment, the greater your chances of producing a product that meets your customer's needs. The more you identify problem areas and develop a plan to take preventative action, the greater your chances of success.

There is, however, a caveat to this thought. Process control plans must be implemented in a way that is as unobtrusive as possible to the process itself. For example, control plans that involve constant operator input, machine tweaking, excessive sampling, and the like can lead to reduced throughput, product variations, and operator frustration. Careful consideration is required, therefore, when establishing a control plan to find the proper balance between control and constriction.

HOW DO I DO IT?

Delivering any product to the marketplace never consists of a single step. Manufacturing operations are collections of a series of smaller events culminating in the final outcome.

The key to process control is the understanding that you must own the process and not allow the process to own you. Many times I have seen hardworking people chasing after a process in order to maintain product quality and consistency. Much time is wasted on the shop floor making adjustments. While this looks like productivity and indeed people are working hard, it is in fact counterproductive and inefficient. A process that needs constant manipulation is a process crying out to be understood.

It should also be noted here that a discussion on best practices for process control makes the assumption that you have already chosen the equipment or machinery with the ability to produce the product you desire. Best practices for process control consist of five fundamentals:

1. Identifying key process variables
2. The control plan
3. Equipment setup/documentation and verification
4. Process capability
5. Monitoring

IDENTIFYING KEY PROCESS VARIABLES

One of the first steps in starting any new process should be the identification of key process variables (KPVs). *Key process variables* may be defined as: *any machine setting, work procedure, or process that will affect the ability of the final output product to meet its quality and performance requirements.*

Identifying all the possible key process variables for a single product is a time-consuming and frustrating endeavor but is a step that cannot be left out. Identification of KPVs is as important a step as making machine selection, calculating cost, or return on investment. Without

KPVs, you are a ship without a map or compass but running full steam to *somewhere*.

Identifying and defining key process variables starts by understanding what attributes and characteristics the product should have after the current or final process step. Some sources that can be of assistance in determining KPVs are:

- End-user customer specifications.
- Input and setup requirements for the next process step.
- List of characteristics discovered during the review for quality requirements.
- The undocumented, yet expected, experience of quality attributes by your final customer. (For example, you expect the tires on your new car should last more than 1,000 miles.)

The output from KPVs should always be measurable. A few examples of this would be product physical dimensions, chemical makeup, appearance, or performance criteria. The reason for requiring the KPV output to be measurable is to allow for the subsequent steps of process capability, verification, and monitoring.

Defining KPVs requires input from all your resources. No one person will have all the information about KPVs. While an industrial engineer may have designed the process and understands the equipment, no one understands the process better than the operator on the floor. When it comes to understanding how to get the most out of your process, the operator who lives with that equipment daily will know it best. Typically, the operator will understand what conditions and settings are required to achieve the desired results. One must also remember, in a multistep process, that the next manufacturing line and its operators are also *customers*. They are the consumers of all previous work. These *internal* customers are invaluable in assisting you to understand what KPVs are required to control the product input for their process.

Therefore, collecting this information from all operators and internal consumers can greatly increase the chances of identifying all the KPVs to manufacture your product. While this entire body of practical knowledge may never find its way into an external customer's final specification, it becomes vital in producing a product that will have the characteristics required.

Gathering information about KPVs can be done in several ways. These include, but are not limited to:

- A formalized specification review of documents from your outside customer with translation into terms or language understandable on your shop floor
- Face-to-face review of requirements with your customer or possibly a visit to its production facilities to gain better understanding of what is required from your product and how it is used
- Small-group meetings internally with participants at all levels from the industrial engineers to operators to convert quality requirements into application settings

Regardless of which methods you use to gather and define KPVs, they are useless unless you have a means to store and disseminate this information. I recommend electronic databases to create a centralized repository containing both the detailed results from your review as well as a summarized list of KPVs derived from those reviews. Working documents for use on the shop floor such as equipment setup sheets and work instructions can then be created through use of this repository.

THE CONTROL PLAN

Now that we have established what we want to manufacture and what variables we need to control in order to produce it, we must now develop the methods or *plan* based on the KPVs. KPVs can, and most likely will, have an effect on each other. Adjusting your process for one KPV to alter one characteristic, such as length, can have detrimental effects on other KPVs like width or diameter. So identifying KPVs is not only about identification of vital settings. Identifying KPVs is also about understanding KPV interactions and making provisions for those interactions in your control plan.

The control plan consists of all the information required to set up and run your equipment so that the equipment will yield a product with the correct attributes. The control plan is the final culmination of our work thus far. The plan should contain, at a minimum, all the manufacturing equipment settings, plus tolerances, operator instructions, quality control sampling, testing protocols, and operator inline quality checks. I cannot stress enough the importance of a thorough understanding of your equipment's controls as they relate to the desired KPV. The concept of *design of experiments* is worth mentioning here as this method allows real-life testing of all permutations of machine settings to KPVs. Simply put, design of experiments requires you to test all possible combinations when *slamming the knobs* on your equipment and reveals the subsequent effect on your product. Many fine books/software are available for understanding design of experiments. I recommend you obtain an understanding of this concept before you begin the design of your process control plan.

■ ■ ■

Now that we have our plan, let's look at setting up our equipment.

EQUIPMENT SETUP/DOCUMENTATION AND VERIFICATION

A best practices process control plan is our blueprint and outline to set up our equipment. The plan may be a printed paper document or electronic. Either method is acceptable as long as it has these two items. The document must contain an area for the machine setup person to sign off on each setting, and the setup document used must be the most current revision. For more on this revision control, see Chapter 6.

No matter the method, the machine settings portion of the plan should be laid out in natural sequential order of how the setup is to take place. This order may come from historical experience, an industrial engineer, or the equipment manufacturer. Equipment settings may affect one another; therefore, the setup sequence matters. As the operator completes each setting or instruction, it is important that the completed section be signed off by the operator when complete. One common error I have seen is that the operator will complete the entire setup and then sign off on every section all at once. This is not a best practice. This practice can allow missing a step by accident. By signing off all at once, the operator is not addressing each specific task at hand but rather *doing the paperwork*. It is important in our operators' training to address the need for the *sign-off-as-completed* approach. The next step is verification.

An incorrect setup in any process carries a certain liability. These liabilities can run the gamut of issues but *all* have a financial impact on your company. Therefore, another best practice is to have a secondary verification of the setup by another operator or supervisor. Verification may also be accomplished by means of *first run and hold*. This verification method consists of running the machine with the current setup and, once the process is stable, taking sample(s) of the product. The equipment is then stopped or slowed until the evaluation of product can be performed. Once the process is making suitable product, the equipment is released to produce at production rates. Any previously produced material made during the verification step may be considered production quality if all properties have been met for the time period that produced them.

PROCESS CAPABILITY

No discussion about process control would be complete without touching on process capability. Simply put, process capability is the determination that the current process, as defined by the KPVs, is statistically able to produce the desired product characteristics. Best practice in this area dictates that process capability be evaluated at the very beginning of every new process and subsequently on a periodic basis during the life of an existing process. Evaluating a new process can be challenging due to the lack of sufficient data. However, it is preferable to run a limited number of trials to gather data in order to get a feel for the potential capability.

Periodic review of process capability should happen for two reasons. First, any time equipment is updated or major parts replaced it is always a good idea to review to ensure the updates or new parts have not caused a shift in process performance. I would not recommend a review for simple maintenance. Second, review is helpful if equipment has been running for a long time without any major changes to ensure that wearing of parts has not created a process shift. The frequency and necessity of these reviews may be altered by evidence from previous reviews over time. For instance, if reviewing process capability with each new major equipment update shows no effect, then major updates no longer trigger a review. This is an acceptable risk. On the contrary, if a review every six months of long-running equipment always reveals a process shift, both the review and equipment maintenance should happen more frequently.

Let's explore the fundamentals of process capability.

An analogy I prefer that spells this out quite well is the *car-on-the-road* example. Let's say you are driving down a single-lane road. Common sense dictates that in order for the car to fit down the road it must not be wider than the road itself. If the car is too wide, both tires are in the ditches and you have no room to maneuver. If your car, however, is only half as wide as the road, there is plenty of room on either side of you to move around.

Consider your process to be the car, and the road represents the product specification you are trying to meet. We must understand that every process has a natural rhythm, an ebb and flow like breathing that is statistically measurable. The width or range of this variation is our car's width. It is the expected variation when all KPV-derived settings are left untouched and the process is allowed to run. We can mathematically make the comparison of this variation to our specifications and derive a value that tells us just how well we are meeting our specifications and what we can expect from our current setup. There are many formulas and statistics for process capability and many good software titles available to calculate and graph this for you.

I prefer to use the statistics *Cp* and *Cpk*. Cp is a ratio measurement of our car's (process) width to the road (specification). A value of 1.0 means both the process and the specification ranges are equal. A value of 0.5 shows our process is twice as wide as the specification—not a good place to be. Our car is wider than the road when the value is 0.5. What we desire is for something greater than 1.0; Cps at this level indicate the process can have room to follow its natural variation while riding within the specification's range or width. A Cp of 2.0, for example, indicates we could fit two cars side-by-side on our road.

While Cp evaluates how much room we have to drive within our process, it does not address where our car (process) is centered right now.

This requires the calculation of a Cpk value. Cpk takes into account both the process variation and where the process is centered. In our car-and-road analogy, we may have a very good Cp that says we have lots of room to steer. But Cpk may tell us that our car (process) is centered along the very edge of one of our specs. In other words, we're driving on the road's shoulder. Half our car is riding in the ditch, the other half on the road. Half the time our process is making out-of-specification material. In a scenario like this, our process variation will take us off the road half the time but gradually swing back completely onto the road sometime in the future and then repeat that cycle. Cpk together with Cp gives us a clear view of both where we are and how much we can move. The goal is to use both statistics to adjust our process in order to align the actual process center point or average with the center of our specification. Knowing these statistics we may work to remove variation from the process in order to obtain the greatest maneuverability and center point control.

One final note about process capability: For any process to be controlled using data-driven statistics such as Cp and Cpk, the data must be normally distributed. This is the old *bell curve* we are all familiar with and is referred to as a *histogram* by most statisticians. This curve shows how the data is distributed and can be thought of as a visual representation of the width of our *car*. A balanced normal histogram will have most of the data elements grouped around the center point or average of the graph. The remaining data elements should be equally distributed on each side of the average in a mirror image of each other. This is in an ideal world. Most often, data will resemble this configuration but not exactly. That's when good statistical software can apply mathematical rules and aid you in deciding if your data is normal.

The point is this: If the data is not normally distributed, you cannot assume that any of the statistics for process capability or control are valid. You must identify and resolve the issues causing the abnormal data before allowing that same data to lead you and your process.

MONITORING

Equipment monitoring takes on many forms depending on the industry. Best practices consist of a feedback system to either the operator or a computerized set of controls. There should never be a *set-it-and-forget-it* approach that assumes the setting is correct without some sort of means to measure that setting.

Much of today's modern manufacturing equipment is under control of logic circuits or software but even these need to be checked periodically and calibration assured. If your system does not use these programmable logic controller (PLC)-type controls, then at the very least have a calibrated readout gauge or monitor that gives some comparison of machine setting to actual process conditions.

Monitoring also consists of a sampling plan for testing of product characteristics. This plan may be based on experience with the product and the understanding of process variation gained during the establishment of the initial control plan. It may also be dictated by customer requirements. If no other guidance is given, you may reference ANSI/ASQC Z1.4/1993, which gives you the minimum required sampling frequency plus accept and reject rates based on units produced. Whatever the method, it is important to monitor product output quality versus KPVs and adjust the process only if necessary. Monitoring also allows for the possible discovery of a missed KPV that manifests itself as an undesirable product attribute. An understanding of control charting and statistical process control is invaluable in monitoring and in assisting in the decision to tweak the process or leave it alone.

FINAL THOUGHTS

As you can now see, process control is a very real example of the old adage, *plan, do, check, act*. By following these minimum fundamentals you are well on your way to producing a quality product that is consistent and meets your customer's needs. In summary, the best practices for process control require:

- Process control must be data driven.
- KPVs are vital to establish a controllable process.
- KPV output must be identified and measurable.
- KPVs are used to define our machine setup protocol.
- Control plan consists of KPVs and details for running the process.
- Process must be monitored for capability, stability, and normality using feedback controls, sampling, testing, and statistics.

CHAPTER **8**

Process Changes

A well-known tire company had just hired a new operator in its rubber compounding department. The new employee was assigned to the night shift and was in charge of the complex task of combining all the various raw ingredients in a huge mixing vat based on a set recipe. Part of his job was submission of a batch sample to quality control. These samples were evaluated for various properties depending on the requirements for the tires being produced. One such test evaluated the ability of the rubber to resist wear. The better the wear strength, the longer tires would last.

After a short time, the lab data showed that the new employee's batches consistently tested with a higher wear strength than any other shift. The company sought to know how this operator, so new to the job, was able to so significantly improve his product. A team of observers was assembled to monitor his every move. Every machine setting and adjustment was carefully noted. Oddly enough, during the observation period, the lab results were back in line with other shifts. Obviously whatever the operator was doing, he wasn't doing it while he was being watched.

Determined to get to the bottom of this, the operator was called in to have a discussion with the company engineers and managers. The operator started the conversation by saying he did not want to be fired if he shared openly. The company officials, eager to know what he was doing, of course agreed.

The new operator, it turns out, enjoyed beer. In fact, he would drink a six-pack of beer every night before coming to work. As anyone knows, consuming large quantities of any liquid, especially beer, invariably creates a need. Not wanting to frequently leave his post, for fear of being discovered, the operator answered nature's call directly into the vat of mixing rubber.

Armed with this information, further testing was conducted and the findings indicated that the trace amounts of uric acid added by the operator had a significant, positive impact on rubber wear strength.

The operator kept his job, after being reminded about the company's alcohol policy. The company changed their rubber recipe to add the uric acid, obtained through proper channels, of course. The operator also received a commendation for product improvement.

This story, unlike other examples in this book, is true. It was told to me by someone who witnessed it. What a great example of the need to document process changes. In this example, a process change made a positive quality improvement that, left undocumented, would have never benefited the company. This time the company was lucky. Not all undocumented process changes have a positive effect. So let's look at how to set up a system to take luck out of the equation.

In manufacturing there is one thing that is always constant and that thing is *change*. Process conditions, raw materials, methods, machinery—the list is endless. In order to survive in the manufacturing world of today, manufacturers must be able to respond quickly to the ever-changing landscape of competition and customer demands. Global economies can change the price or availability of raw materials in the blink of an eye. Newer, faster equipment becomes available on a regular basis. A new procedure that is more effective and less wasteful is developed and put in place. A corrective action requires implementation.

We want to optimize our business. We desire to take advantage of new equipment and ideas. We need to embrace change in order to stay alive in the marketplace. How do we accomplish these goals while at the same time avoiding internal chaos, confusion, or the consequences of making a change that was not well thought out or communicated? Once again, we need a system.

Simply put, a Process Change Control system is a controlled, centralized clearing house of all, *and I do mean all*, changes to the status quo of your entire operation. Whereas this system can be created manually, it is best designed utilizing a computerized database due to the amount of data, the voting process, and handling of task completion dates. For the sake of this discussion we shall assume a database system is the solution of choice.

Responsibility for management of the Process Change Control system is typically relegated to a nonpartisan authority such as quality control or quality assurance. This third-party regulation helps the system run more smoothly by creating a single contact point for the bidirectional flow of information. Third-party management also allows for screening of submitted change requests for completeness and clarity before change requests are circulated within the company for approvals.

Although managed by the quality area, this does not mean the system is inaccessible to everyone else. The system must be designed to be available to any individual authorized to initiate a request or vote on a pending change. Let's look more in depth at what we mean by *change*.

By now you should have a good idea that manufacturing best practices is entirely dependent on documentation, paper or otherwise, procedures, and multiple systems that control all facets of your operations. These elements of documentation and systems, taken as an integrated whole, become your *standards of practice.* Any deviation from this set of standardized practices has the potential to change your final product quality or cost of manufacturing.

When changes are made we must be absolutely sure of two things: First, we must fully understand the effect of the proposed change by gathering as much information, from as many sources or people, as possible. Second, we must establish and keep a history or pedigree of all changes that becomes a ready reference in the event of a quality issue. The Process Change Control system, therefore, becomes the *master system* overseeing changes to all the other systems, procedures, and documentation.

The ultimate goal of the Process Change Control system is to strictly regulate any and all changes made to our current practices. The system requires the change to be reviewed and approved by multiple individuals within the company. Typically no one individual within a company has total knowledge of all the interrelations between process, material, and product quality. No one can know all the possible outcome scenarios. Therefore we must use the collective understanding from all areas of the business in order to be sure the change has the desired effect. All parties with a vested interest must agree to, and approve, the change. A *single disapproval* shall be enough to prevent further action.

Now that we understand that changes in our operations must be undertaken in a controlled way, let's look at the data components required to design our database system. We will also look at each component in detail to understand why it is needed.

REQUEST SUBMISSION

The change approval process begins with the submission of the idea or request. At the core of the Process Change Control system is the process change request input form. This document or screen is our starting point and contains all the information regarding the proposed change. At a minimum, the change request form includes:

- Unique request number
- Name and title of requester
- Name and title of request initiator
- Date of request
- The affected areas, departments, locations
- The process, procedure, documents, or material affected by the change
- Goal of the change, such as quality, safety, process improvement, or cost reduction (if applicable)
- Complete details of the change itself, including the current condition and proposed new condition and including any draft documents or drawing changes
- Reason for the change, including any supporting evidence from trial work or process deviations showing the effect of change or other justification

This is enough information to initiate the change request process. However, this is not enough information to circulate the request for approval, monitor its progress, or indicate its approval status. For that, we need to add more information to our system:

- Approval status of the request and date
- Who needs to approve the change?
- Who actually makes the change?
- Has the change been made, and if so, what was the effective date?
- Who needs to be notified about the change once it is approved?
- Is training required for personnel after change is implemented?

REQUEST SUBMISSION ◀ 97

- Does the change need follow-up for effectiveness once implemented? If so, what is the due date and date completed of follow-up?
- Results of the follow-up
- Completion status of the change request

This is quite a lot of information and may look like overkill. Let's review each component and discuss the rationale behind inclusion in our system.

Unique Identification

Once the decision is made to use a change control system to track and approve *all* changes, the requests will start rolling in. It quickly becomes apparent that there are lots of changes happening. Even in smaller companies, the sheer number of items changed on a daily basis can become overwhelming. The volume of requests dictates we have a method to uniquely identify each one. So, the very first step in processing a request is the assignment of a tracking identification. It doesn't matter whether this identification is a number, letters, or some combination of the two; it simply must be unique to that single request.

Name and Title of Requester

This is the name and title of the person making the request. This information is necessary in the event we need more information or clarification or have questions. The original requester may or may not be the person who is submitting the change form. Often requests flow down from upper managers to subordinates for submission. Therefore, we need to know who actually originated the request in order to provide feedback when the change is either approved or rejected.

Name and Title of Request Initiator

As previously mentioned, this person may or may not be the same as the original requester. This is the name and title of the person actually entering the request into the system. In the event of a question or possible error, it is necessary to know who actually entered the data. If this person is not the original requester, then she is acting as a translation agent for the original requester, in which case the agent becomes our source for verification and clarification when questions arise.

Affected Areas or Departments

In this section we define the scope of the change. Some changes are global, affecting the entire company, whereas others are more localized and may affect only one process or document. We need to know where the change will have impact and thereby determine who needs to review and approve the change.

During the design phase for our system we shall create responsibility assignments to individuals for each operational area. Linked to each area in turn are all the documents, procedures, and processes. These links then allow us to generate an approval list for all changes in a particular area. Inclusion in our system of the affected area or department becomes the key to our approval list.

Process, Procedure, Documents, or Material Affected by the Change

If we desire to change something in our operation, then we must identify what documents or processes need updating. If we are utilizing best practices for process and document control, we already have in place uniquely named processes, procedures, documents, and materials. In this section of the change system we need to identify, by name, which procedures, processes, and so on are to be changed. Linked to these documents, as mentioned in the previous subsection, are the individuals who own and are responsible for approval of the changes.

Goal of the Change (e.g., Quality, Safety, Process Improvement, or Cost Reduction)

The information contained in this section is not vital to processing the change request. However, many best practices companies set improvement goals in these areas. One way to measure progress toward those goals is to monitor change activity. Categorizing each change request allows for easier summaries and review. A simple category list that can be flagged is enough to capture this data.

Complete Details of the Change

This section contains the bulk of our information. Here we describe our proposed change in detail. These details should include the current condition and the proposed new condition. A simple example entry may read as follows:

Update document for process XYZ and change all control knob settings from 1.5 to 3.0.

By stating both the before and after conditions we create a complete historical record of the change. Logging these details in their own section allows for easier searching should the need arise. Also consider designing your change system to allow for the attachment of scanned documents, pictures, or drawings. With this added feature you may further supplement your request by showing current documents alongside marked-up draft copies, helping to clarify the request where words fail to describe.

Reason for the Change

Obviously the old adage, "If it ain't broke, don't fix it," can apply here. We would never change a process without a valid reason. In this section we log in a detailed explanation of why we are requesting the change. Include details, history, and any supporting evidence from trial work or process deviations that justifies the decision for permanent change.

Here are two possible examples:

1. *Recent customer complaint and rejection of 10,000 units due to improper packaging requires revision of packaging instructions.*

2. *Capability analysis of process data shows equipment settings not producing product within specification limits. Trials run under temporary*

deviations show new settings correct the problem. See attached scanned control charts. Equipment settings procedure requires update to new settings to bring process in control.

The change reason coupled with the details from the previous sections provides our approval group a clear view of the situation, the proposed solution, and justification for our request.

Approval Status of the Request

A change request actually has several phases of life. These are:

- **Draft.** Change request has unique identification assigned but is still being updated with information and has not been submitted for review by control authority.
- **Submitted.** Request has been sent to control authority for review and distribution to approval group.
- **Awaiting approval.** Request is circulating among the approval group for voting.
- **Final approval or rejection.** Results of approval voting. Request is either approved or rejected.

Designing your system to include request status indicators facilitates system management. In an operation where many change requests are circulating simultaneously we need a way to know the status of any single request at any given time. Status indicators also allow for search and grouping functions to monitor requests so that we may take action on any request that is beyond its voting due date.

Who Needs to Approve the Change?

Obviously, since every change must be voted upon, we need a list of individuals who have the knowledge required to vote. Building this list encompasses most of the preparation work for our system. We lightly touched on this idea of voter lists in a previous subsection, "Affected Areas or Departments."

Each controlled process, procedure, or document object you create must have an individual person who is responsible for the object's content and accuracy. This designated individual becomes the controlled object's owner. In turn, these objects may be used and understood by many other users throughout your organization. Although these users do not possess control authority for the object, they do possess knowledge about, or experience with, the object. These users are vital to ensuring any changes made to the object are correct. Our voter list must include these individuals as well.

Creating this list for each controlled object is painstaking. Who needs to vote to approve a change is often the source of great debates within a company. The time to craft this list is well spent, however, for it ensures we have collectively assessed the change correctly and the change will yield the outcome we desire.

Who Actually Makes the Change?

This may sound like redundant information. Didn't we just discuss the idea that every controlled object has an owner? It seems likely that this person would be the one to create the updates. This is not necessarily so. The object's owner holds responsibility to see changes are made but the actual work may be performed by someone else.

For example, take a manufacturing operation where thousands of drawings are used every day. Responsibility for the drawings falls on the design manager. Working with the design manager is a team of a dozen engineers who actually create and publish the drawings. The manager is responsible for the drawing and most likely is on the approval list for changes. Once approved, however, one engineer actually makes the change and distributes the drawing.

So in the design of our database we need to provide space to input the identity of the person actually making the change. This allows for direct notification of any newly approved changes and expedites the update process.

Has the Change Been Made? If So, What Was the Effective Date?

This data element of our database is for tracking purposes only and helps us keep the Process Change Control system running efficiently.

As a control measure we need to be sure all approved updates are completed in a timely manner. This data element is a simple yes-or-no flag on our database. The flag will allow quick scanning or report grouping to provide a status list of approvals and help follow-up on delinquent updates. The effective date of change is also captured for tracking purposes and as a historical record. There is more on the use of dates at the end of this chapter.

Who Needs to Be Notified about the Change Once It Is Approved?

We have already discussed the qualifications for individuals who are required to vote and approve changes. These people have the knowledge or job position to authorize such changes. This group is our voters.

Outside our voting group lies another collection of people who are the consumers of the information. These are people without voting privileges who use the documents or objects in their daily routine. It is these people who are the final recipients of the changes. Therefore, we need to create another list of individuals to be notified once the changes are approved. Compiling this list can be done concurrently with creation of our voter list.

Is Training Required for Personnel after Change Is Implemented?

Making changes that affect our standard practices often requires training of our employees in the new methods. Our database should capture this requirement by use of a yes-or-no flag. The flag can then be used as a trigger point to our training system to begin the education process once the change is implemented.

Does the Change Need Follow-up for Effectiveness Once Implemented?

We covered the goals of the change, such as quality, safety, process improvement, or cost reduction, in an earlier subsection. For these types of goals it is necessary to evaluate how effective the change was in achieving the desired outcome. Initiation of the evaluation is the concern here, not how the evaluation is undertaken. Again, the yes-or-no flag can help us. Inclusion of this flag allows us to identify changes needing follow-up evaluation and to notify the appropriate people to conduct that follow-up.

If effectiveness follow-up is needed, it is also a good idea to include both the due date and date completed in our database to track the evaluation progress.

Results of the Follow-Up

Obviously, if we conduct the follow-up evaluation, then we should record the details of our findings along with the rest of our change data. Use scanned documents attached to the affected change request if the results are too large to enter into a database format. Otherwise, creating a space in the database to record our results should be sufficient.

Completion Status of the Change Request

Each request should have an indication of completion. Put simply, Is the request still an open issue for voting or pending document updates, or has it been approved with all training and follow-up completed? Include an *open* or *closed* flag on the database to indicate the status. This flag also gives us the ability to better manage the system by acting as a filter to group requests with like statuses.

Dates

You will notice that this system tracks dates for many of the components—dates for initiation, approval, document changes, follow-up, and so on. These various dates allow us to calculate the amount of time taken to complete the various steps for a change request. This time difference, or cycle time, is a direct indication of the speed at which we can respond to and implement change. Since one of our goals is to respond quickly to change or customer requests, cycle time calculations are an indicator of our success. I recommend inclusion of the cycle time reports on your system where they are viewable by everyone. Publishing summarized reports by manufacturing location or department can be a great motivator for cycle time reduction. Cycle time reduction may also be made into a valid quality objective.

EXTERNAL COMMUNICATION OF CHANGES

Our system design thus far addresses only the internal processes of voting, notification, and approval. Many times the changes we make affect outside sources such as material suppliers or customers.

Changes made to how our products are manufactured can have detrimental effects for an unaware customer. Smart final customers will build a provision for change notification or approval into their product specifications to address this issue. However, if change notification to customers is not dictated by specification or law, notification becomes an internal business decision. When in doubt about notification, consider your options carefully while remembering that transparency with your customers is always the best option.

In a best practices operation, raw materials are sourced using signed-off, mutually agreed specifications. Raw material suppliers should, at the very least, be notified when we make changes to our incoming product specifications. At best, the supplier should be included in your voting group with approval authority.

The decision to extend process change voting or notifications outside your organization is up to you. If you decide to do so, include some indicator in your change system design to flag this requirement.

FINAL THOUGHTS

All changes are aimed at improvement of your business operations or product quality. The need for change is sometimes within our control and sometimes forced by outside conditions. Uncontrolled change is the enemy here, not change itself. The creation of a database system, built with all the elements we have discussed, is your best assurance that the changes you make are based on solid evidence and experience. The system assures that all the right people are involved in a change decision, democratizes the handling of changes, and gleans the experience and knowledge from our experts.

Our final product here is not only a control device for change but a historical archive—an archive that contains the entire chain of events, people, and thought processes in use at a particular point in time. This time capsule is an invaluable resource for research of issues and as a guide for future changes. Possession of a Process Change Control system and the ability to establish a pedigree for changes is another core best practice.

CHAPTER **9**

Raw Materials, Services, and Suppliers

There was a tale I remember hearing as a child about the old man who asked his son the builder to build him a house.

The old man said, "My son, I am not long for this world and I'm not very rich. All my life I wanted to live in a fine home with all the luxuries others have enjoyed. You have so much. You have been fortunate to make a better living than I by building houses. I am asking you, out of your love for me, to build a house for me that is finer than any in town. Design it however you wish for I completely trust you. I will not interfere with the work and will only come see the house once it is finished."

The son, not being as virtuous as his father, agreed to the idea but was not inclined to give away his money so easily. He bought the cheapest materials he could find. He hired the least skilled labor possible and paid them little. He used shoddy construction methods and cut corners wherever possible. The son was clever despite his poor ethics. Most of the money he spent was on completely cosmetic façades. The house had no real internal substance but looked every bit a mansion on the inside and out.

The day came when the house was completed. The old man's eyes gleamed as he saw the magnificent structure before him. The son handed the keys to his dad, who unlocked the front door. They strolled from room to room admiring the son's deceptive handiwork.

The old man turned to his son, took him by the hand, and gently placed the keys there.

"This is the only thing of value I've ever had in my life. I feared I would not have anything for you to inherit when I die. Now, I do. Son, this house is yours."

A great story with a great moral that can be applied to our world of manufacturing. We must be careful not to cut corners when we source our materials and services. The only one we cheat may be ourselves.

Manufacturing begins with raw materials. The final quality of the products you produce can be no better than the quality of the raw materials you start with. The old computer programmer's adage, *garbage in, garbage out,* also applies here. Likewise, the quality of any services you purchase that touches the production of your product affects its quality as well. Based on these premises, common sense dictates we have strong measures in place for sourcing, purchasing, verifying, and tracking the quality of raw materials and services.

SOURCING: RAW MATERIALS

There are many facets to evaluating raw material sources. Take care to avoid the common error made by many companies in basing this critical decision *solely on price*. What you save on the raw material price can wind up costing you more in the long run. While acknowledging price as a major factor in our source decision, it should be our last, not first, priority. Let's review all the considerations, including cost, when sourcing raw materials.

Availability

It does not matter how well a supplier can meet your raw material requirements if their product is not available when you need it. This is especially true for specialty materials not considered commodity items. You need to request, and document, your supplier's protocol for stocking enough material to fill your orders as they arrive. If the material cannot be stocked but must be manufactured, the lead time required for production must be known. Lead time from order receipt to delivery is critical to your manufacturing planning.

The evaluation must also include discussion of the supplier's output capacity. You must ensure the supplier's ability to produce meets or exceeds your consumption rate. It is also a good practice to discuss and document contingency plans in the event your supplier suffers a catastrophic failure. How will your supplier meet your needs if the supplier's manufacturing facility were damaged or destroyed due to accident or natural disaster? This last question sounds extreme, but when choosing a supplier you need to consider how *you* will stay in business should the supplier fail to have product available. Up-front discussions such as these force you to consider your own plans should a supplier flounder. Remember, the last thing you want to do is start sourcing materials in an emergency situation.

Delivery

Delivery is not the same as availability but they are related. It does not matter if your supplier can produce sufficient amounts of a product if he cannot get it to you in a timely fashion. Many modern manufacturing facilities utilize the *Just in Time (JIT)* approach for incoming raw materials. If you are unfamiliar with this concept, JIT is a delivery method coordinated with military-like precision. Rarely, if ever, are any raw materials stocked locally at the manufacturing site. Rather, the production areas are fed by raw material deliveries that arrive on the dock just as the last of the current material is about to be consumed. JIT is a tremendous cost saver if you can incorporate it into your operations.

Even if JIT cannot be used, timely deliveries of raw materials are crucial to your operations. As you evaluate and negotiate with material suppliers keep the following questions in mind:

- What are the various transportation methods used by the supplier to ship its product?
- What is the supplier's preferred method: truck, rail, air, or ocean freighter, and so on?
- How does the delivery method affect the cost?
- May we choose our own transportation method and provider?
- Are there any restrictions on shipping days such as weekdays only or holidays?

■ What are the names of the companies supplying transportation services?

■ How are these transportation providers chosen by the supplier?

■ How is delivery performance of transportation providers measured and tracked?

■ Is performance data about on-time delivery and damage issues available for review?

■ Is there a list of current customers we may contact to discuss their experience with your delivery methods?

Obviously this line of questioning is an attempt to build a clear picture of the supplier's ability to deliver. Even if our supplier candidate has the best product on the planet, it is worthless if he cannot deliver it when needed. We must have a comfort level that our supplier has already sorted out any issues around the prompt delivery of their product. This comfort level is built on hard facts, honest conversations, and open negotiations.

Material Source Location: Domestic or Offshore

A major factor affecting availability, delivery, and price is the geographic origin of the raw materials. The choice of where to source your raw materials is a business management decision and there are no set rules for choosing between domestic or offshore sourcing. Raw materials define such a wide scope of products I can offer only some generic thoughts for consideration.

If you source your materials offshore, you must take into account and plan for:

■ Extended lead and shipping time

■ Questionable or inconsistent quality

■ Price variations due to fluctuating money exchange rates and fuel costs

■ Difficulty and expense in returning noncompliant material

■ Difficulty and expense of onsite audit at supplier's location

■ Availability disruption due to political or social issues

- Increased cost for holding a local supply of buffer inventory in the event of supply disruption
- Economic impact of sending money and jobs offshore

Domestic sourcing can be affected by:

- Inadequate domestic supply to meet demand, especially if raw material is from natural resources
- Availability disruption due to labor disputes
- Price fluctuations due to fuel costs
- Availability and price affected by environmental regulations

The choice here is not a simple one. The only best practice I can suggest is to carefully weigh your options against these concerns when planning your supplier strategies.

Openness to Audit

Up to this point our raw material sourcing has been an investigative venture. We have asked questions, perhaps reviewed some documents, and negotiated delivery requirements. All this work is building toward creation of a document—a *raw material product specification* that can be signed by both the supplier and ourselves. Before the document can be finalized, however, there is one more vital discussion we must have with our candidate supplier. Our supplier must be open to the idea of allowing us to audit his operations, as needed, to ensure all requirements of the specification can be met.

Some suppliers may have quality systems in place that are certified to a known standard such as ISO 9000. These suppliers may offer you their certification as evidence that their quality system is capable of meeting your requirements. The decision to solely accept such a certification without audits is a business decision you should be prepared to make. Even with the presence of such certificates, I still recommend the right to conduct audits be included in your negotiated specification.

I include the idea of audits at this point because it can be a real deal breaker. A supplier, certified or not, that will not allow verification of all agreed-upon requirements is a liability to your operations and should not be used. If this situation exists, there is no need to move any further in negotiations or for the creation of the product specification.

Quality

Quality has different meanings to different people. Just as our customers have expectations of our product's performance, so do we have expectations of our raw materials. Purchasing raw material specifications are an absolute must for any business transaction between you and your supplier. Any supplier under consideration who will not agree to sign off on an agreed-upon specification should be immediately removed as a candidate. Without agreed and signed specifications in place, you, your operation, and your product quality are at the mercy of your supplier. Worse yet, so are your customers, as there is no guarantee, outside of intensive internal testing, to ensure final product quality.

Purchasing specifications must be developed with input from all functional areas within your organization. The document you produce must include all the quality elements, such as physical and functional requirements, packaging, documentation, and so on. These supplier quality requirements contain most of the same elements as the requirements for our final product. (See the Appendix for more details). In addition to the quality requirements, your purchasing specification should contain the aforementioned detailed information on availability, delivery, and auditing.

Finally, you should include in your specification the requirement for a certificate of compliance for each shipment you receive. The certificate of compliance must be signed by the supplier's authorized quality agent and include batch or lot numbers for the shipment plus any test results to prove specification compliance. If your supplier cannot provide the certificate, then you must be prepared to internally evaluate the quality of each shipment received through testing and inspection procedures.

Price

At last we come to price. Of course, we wish to get the lowest raw material price; the lower the price, the higher the profit margin. What we do not want is the *cheapest* raw materials. Cheapest, by this definition, means poor purity, function, consistency, or any other quality aspect of the materials.

During your price negotiations do not forget to ask for quantity breaks or rebates. Purchase price for a large quantity of material should always be cheaper than the price for smaller orders. These quantity breaks typically apply to a single order and delivery. If you cannot afford, or are not able to use, enough material to meet the quantity break minimum, then ask about rebates. Suppliers often offer rebate incentives once your overall consumption reaches a given threshold for a given time period such as a calendar year. You then receive back a portion of your purchase price. Make rebates and quantity breaks a significant part of your supplier decision.

SOURCING: SERVICES

There are times when it is cheaper to outsource parts of your manufacturing operations. Cheaper cost, infrequent need, and lack of internal capability are often reasons for using these outside services. I recently witnessed a perfect example of this while touring a small winery. As the tour guide was showing us the fermentation tanks and wine presses, I noticed there was no equipment to get the wine into the bottles. Clearly the bottling was happening, but how? Our guide told us once they have all the wine ready to bottle, they have an outside company bring in a mobile bottling plant. This mobile plant is totally contained within the trailer of an 18-wheel tractor-trailer. The wine is bottled in the vineyard's own bottles and in a few days the mobile plant just drives away.

It's a brilliant solution for this startup winery. The cost of outsourcing is far cheaper than installation of expensive equipment that would be used only a few times a year and the mobile solution provided a capability that was missing internally.

Now our winery example may or may not make good financial sense as a permanent solution but it illustrates how there can be occasions where we can benefit from outsourced services. In your manufacturing operations you may outsource such things as process equipment repair and maintenance, instrument calibration, computer systems upgrades, testing, or hiring temporary employees to fill seasonal positions. Each of these outsourced operations will either directly touch your final product quality or impact your customer's quality experience. Knowing this, it is vital that we put as much effort into securing the best services as we did for raw materials.

The process for the sourcing of services involves most of the same elements as raw materials. We still need to be concerned with availability, on-time delivery, location, quality, auditing, and pricing. It is simply more difficult to solidify requirements in these areas as there is no physical product involved. Our decision to select our service vendor will need to somehow address these areas and we will finalize all these details into a signed written specification document or purchasing agreement.

Let's look further into sourcing services.

Availability

Obviously, a service that is not available when we need it is not very useful. Services are sometimes needed long term or temporarily but on very short notice. Be certain to ascertain your candidate service provider's ability to meet your availability requirements by asking questions such as: How much advanced notice is required? Are contracts available that guarantee service priority? If so, what is the minimum contract length? Is there 24-hour availability and, if so, how quickly can they respond?

The idea is to understand the flexibility of your service provider to supply assistance when called. This allows you to better schedule your manufacturing operations in situations requiring such assistance.

On-Time Delivery

This section may not seem necessary at first glance. Just like raw materials, it is of no value for services to be available if the provider cannot perform them on a timely basis. If you outsource your calibration, for instance, and the service provider takes a week to do a procedure that should take a day, your operation is running blind without its instruments for this time. This situation can have a dire impact on your quality.

Perhaps you must bring your equipment down for maintenance and you allow for this downtime in your production schedule. The maintenance service provider takes twice as long as necessary to complete the job. Now your schedule is behind and orders are late to your customers. This is not the ideal situation.

During the evaluation of new service providers ask them to show documented evidence of their ability to delivery on time. A service candidate who is already on top of his business will already have this information and proudly offer it without your having to ask. A candidate who doesn't understand what you are asking for is a candidate you should remove from consideration.

Location

The service provider's location directly affects the time required for delivery and cost depending on the type of service rendered. Using calibration again as an example, suppose we need to send instruments across the country to the supplier's lab. We must consider the production impact of the round-trip transit time or weigh the financial burden from the cost of overnight delivery. In this case, a locally based supplier with mobile capabilities would be the better choice. You will also need to consider the added cost of travel expenses for any supplier who must come on-site. Your best choice, whenever possible, is to source your services from providers located as close to your operations as possible.

In other situations, such as outsourced computer services or human resource assistance, the supplier does not need to be physically present nor any physical items exchanged. Suppliers can work remotely. This expands our pool of candidates for these types of services beyond local constraints, giving us more opportunity to select the best candidate.

Do not skip this step in your evaluation. A supplier who is the least expensive, yet too far away to service you quickly, is a liability, not an asset. Inability to conveniently make use of the supplier's services has obvious repercussions on operational efficiency, cost effectiveness, and quality.

Quality

Ascertaining the quality of services is far more difficult than for raw materials. Usually there is no property to measure. The quality of services is the summation of all previous steps we have examined. Availability, delivery, and location all combine together to create the quality experience expression.

If the service you intend to purchase has measurable items, then be sure to discuss them with your candidate. Let the candidate know you will be tracking such items as error rates, tardiness in appointments, or reworked repairs.

One last step you should take in the evaluation process is to ask for a reference list of prior customers. If the candidate cannot, or will not, provide such a list, remove him from consideration. Again, candidates who are successful in their fields will likely offer this information up front.

With list in hand, take the time to call several of these references and inquire about their experience with the candidate. I find it best to prepare a list of questions ahead of time for these inquiries. The list contains questions that rank the service on a standard scale. For instance:

> On a scale of one to ten, with one being poor and ten being perfect, how would you rate the quality of this supplier's repair work? Using the same scale, how would you rate the candidate's customer service?

Using a standard set of ranked questions allows me to have consistency in my interviews with prior customers and gives me a scorecard based on real numbers. These scorecards are then compared and weigh heavily in my final decision.

Auditing and Pricing

Clearly, auditing a service provider is more of a challenge than a raw material supplier. Audits for service providers are more focused around documentation and operational procedures as opposed to production of a physical product. Service providers should allow you to audit at their site to review work instructions, customer complaint protocols, corrective action procedures, and overall quality system structure. As with raw material suppliers, service providers not open to being audited should not be considered as candidates for your business.

Pricing services can be more challenging than raw materials since there are no physical quantities involved. Competition in your area, or the lack thereof, also drives pricing options. This does not mean, however, that we do not have negotiating points that allow us to get the best price. Ask about service contract costs versus *as-needed* pricing. Inquire about long-term contracts and exclusivity agreements. Most service providers will offer discounts to customers who are willing to make contractual agreements as this represents a stable income for the supplier. Arrangements like these represent a win-win situation for both parties.

Decision Time

If you have successfully evaluated your suppliers using the previous steps, you should be able to rank them in order of ability to meet your needs. Now you have evidence on which to base your pricing decision. If two or more candidates have similar rankings, deciding to use the least expensive supplier makes sense. However, if one candidate far outranks all the others, but costs a bit more, choose that one. The concept here is to choose the supplier with the best price for your company who can also meet or exceed all the requirements of your quality system.

Along with choosing your primary supplier comes the decision about sourcing multiple suppliers for the same goods or services. The best practice for choosing suppliers should always include a backup plan. In your sourcing efforts always try to qualify more than one candidate and include them on your approved sources list for use in case of emergencies.

AFTER SOURCING: THE START OF A NEW RELATIONSHIP

Congratulations, you now have a brand new supplier for your raw materials or services. So what is next? Just jump right in and begin purchasing, right? No; as with any new relationship, we proceed with guarded caution. We shall take steps to ensure our new business partners live up to their promises and our expectations. Let's look at how we might accomplish this.

Raw Materials

We have an agreement with our supplier and a jointly signed specification. We are now ready to begin purchasing and receiving raw materials. At this point in time our newly formed vendor–supplier relationship is untried and untested. We need to have trust that our supplier can deliver the quality materials we agreed on but that trust must be built. There are two solutions to this problem. One is the *certificate of compliance*, where the supplier certifies, or guarantees, the materials meet specification. The other is internal testing of each incoming shipment when certificates are not available. Let's look more closely at these options.

Are you going to receive and release your new raw materials to production areas solely based on the supplier's signed certificate of compliance? The short answer is, "No." We must *trust but verify*.

The only way to build our trust in the certificate of compliance is to establish in-house testing of samples from the new supplier. The samples may be taken from received shipments or, better yet, require your supplier to send pre-shipment samples for your approval and release before your order can be delivered. Regardless of which sampling method you choose, in-house testing for compliance against the raw material specification is crucial when beginning to use a new supplier.

During the new material supplier search, plan for the expense and labor required for this internal testing. Do not short-change yourself on this decision. You must be certain your raw materials exactly meet your needs. You also have to ensure that a critical material property was not incorrectly communicated or mistakenly omitted during the specification creation. If any issues like these exist, they will likely surface very early during incoming testing.

Once sufficient testing is completed to allow trust in the certificate, you may decide to test less often, or not at all, and rely completely on the supplier's documentation. Once you are comfortable with the accuracy of the certificate, you may release subsequently received material directly into your process provided the shipment documentation is in order. However, since you are already set up to perform testing in-house, I advocate continued testing on a reduced frequency to audit the supplier's quality level and documentation accuracy.

On the other hand, if certificates of conformance are not available, then you must continue to the next step and internally test each shipment for conformance. This means you will also need to establish sampling frequencies, quarantine, and release procedures.

Raw material received without certifications cannot be directly issued to production areas. These shipments must be identified and isolated to prevent use until quality is verified. One method is to physically segregate these materials in a locked cage or warehouse holding area with limited access. In addition, it is also good practice to label the material containers with a visual reference to indicate their release status. Large red labels with wording such as HOLD—DO NOT USE PENDING QC RELEASE is a good example. Placing labels like these on each container and physically separating them from production materials is the best way to avoid use until tested.

Now that our new shipment is secured we need to test for incoming quality. For this we need a sampling plan. There is no standard plan for every manufacturing operation due to the vast array of raw materials in use in today's industry. The frequency for this plan is best set by your quality control group and customized for your operations. Given no other guidance, a good minimal plan would be to sample and test each incoming lot or batch. If this minimum plan is too lenient, then sample each package received.

The end result of testing will be the final material disposition. The incoming lots are either approved and released to production or rejected and returned. Material found satisfactory should have another label applied showing its released status. Continuing with our previous label example, a green label with wording such as RELEASED BY QC would suffice. I recommend placement of the release label *over the hold label but not totally obscuring it*. Placement of both labels in the clear causes confusion. Which one is current and correct? Placement of *released* labels over *hold* labels makes it easy to see that the container was on hold but is now released. Finally, move your newly released inventory from its quarantine area and into production.

However, if the material is found to be out of compliance, labels should be affixed showing REJECTED, DO NOT USE, RETURN TO VENDOR, or similar wording. Again, placement of rejection labels over the hold label indicates current status. These materials should remain in the quarantine area until such time they can be returned.

This quarantine, test, and release procedure should remain in place until such time a supplier can provide certifications that can be verified.

Services

Verification of services is not quite as easy as raw materials. You can only examine the results of the service and the quality of the service performance itself. Each new service provider you use should be placed on a period of probation. New providers should remain on probation until such time as you can verify the provider demonstrates the ability to perform consistent quality service. These verifications must be conducted in a consistent and organized fashion and not based on opinion or personal feelings.

A good method for organized verification is to create a written procedure that provides detailed instructions for conducting the post-service evaluation. The procedure should contain a checklist of critical attributes that are to be reviewed. Most likely you will find it necessary to create one of these checklists for each type of service vendor you use. The checklist should include tangible items taken directly from your purchasing specification that can be directly measured or qualitatively ranked.

Items for this checklist will vary by service and whether service is performed on or offsite. In addition to the specification requirements, your list should cover other items such as:

- Did provider keep appointments and arrive on time?
- Was the service completed on time and on budget?
- What was the actual date and time of the service and actual total cost?

- Total time taken for service versus quoted time.

- Was equipment returned on time if sent offsite for service?

- Was the work area left clean and as found?

- Were safety protocols followed?

- Were old parts returned if replaced?

- Did service affect product quality or production rates? If so, how?

- List of any equipment physical characteristics, product properties, or system attributes that can be checked.

- Was documentation from service provider in order and complete? This may be further broken down to require inclusion of actual data and detailed service notes as outlined in the specification.

This checklist then becomes the basis for feedback to your service provider and proof of compliance against your service purchase agreement.

Once created, the verification procedure should be performed by someone in your organization following each service event. In cases where the service provider is onsite, you may wish to consider having one of your own employees perform the verification while working alongside the provider. In this way, your employee acts as witness to the provider's methods, work habits, and adherence to specification requirements. I recommend real-time verification only while the provider is in the probationary period.

FINAL THOUGHTS

Beyond sourcing, specifications, and verification, there are two final concepts that round out this discussion: (1) We must be able to externally communicate to suppliers about their performance, and (2) we need to internally control which suppliers are used for materials and services.

Performance Review

Vendor performance review can take the form of scorecards, periodic meetings, or onsite audits at the vendor's location. Whatever the method chosen, the review should be based on, and include, actual measurements from testing, verification checklist findings, and audit results. The goal here is not to air grievances or give perfunctory pats on the back. Honest, cooperative dialog, based on facts, has the goal of giving our suppliers valuable information that can be used for improvement opportunities that are mutually beneficial.

Approved Vendor List

All the effort to source the best suppliers is wasted if your organization does not have a means to prevent using suppliers that have not been through the screening process. For example, if a manager decides she needs to have equipment serviced, she might simply pick up the phone and contact the first listing in the phone book. While this behavior seems sensible, it must be discouraged. Creation of an approved supplier list gives your organization a single centralized contact resource for vendor information. Only suppliers on the approved list are authorized for use.

While the list alone gives guidance it does not ensure its use. The best method to ensure using only approved suppliers is to integrate the approved list with your purchase order system. Such a connection should prevent issuance of a purchase order for materials or services from anyone not on the list. This technique builds the discipline into our systems, not our employees.

■ ■ ■

With these two final pieces in place we can be confident we have a robust system for sourcing and controlling our raw materials and services. We have created a solid method for feedback on quality improvements and are manufacturing top-quality products for our customers using the finest materials and services available.

CHAPTER **10**

Customers

The HelpUComp (HUC) computer company was the newest player in the personal computer market. HUC set itself a corporate goal to provide the highest quality computers in the world, made from the finest raw materials available, and manufactured using the very best practices. These new computers were designed with capabilities not yet seen in the consumer market. HUC was set to revolutionize personal computing.

New manufacturing facilities were built that used the latest state-of-the-art equipment and manufacturing processes. Producing this next evolution in computing also meant that the price-per-unit for its product would be double that of anything currently available. While higher prices meant lower volume of units sold, the profit margin was better on the new computers than on anything else in its product line. HUC believed consumers would be willing to pay more to own the very latest and best, so the higher prices would not be a problem.

HUC based all its belief in customer satisfaction solely on the product and the pride of ownership. HUC gave only cursory thought to handling customer issues. After all, these new computers were so well designed, constructed, and tested, what could go wrong? This short-sighted thinking led HUC to the decision to use its existing call centers, help-desk facilities, and employees for support of this new product.

Predictably, the new computers were well received. Unpredictably, HUC sold record numbers of units in the first few months. Then, the calls starting coming in. It turns out these new computers were so unlike anything on the market, users were struggling to understand and use all the new features. The help desk was completely

123

overwhelmed with telephone calls and online inquiries. Users encountered long waits to talk to a representative or days before e-mail was answered. HUC had underestimated the importance of prompt customer service.

News soon spread that HUC had a great new expensive toy on the market, but its customer service was so poor no one would recommend buying one. Market share soon dropped as customers rejected the idea of paying a premium price for a product with no support. HUC missed the most vital of best practices: Customer service *always* comes first.

Of course this story is fictional and certainly most modern manufacturers would not be this short sighted. The story stands, however, as testament to the idea that customer service and our customer's experience of doing business with us is, and must be, our first priority.

Manufacturers have no reason to exist without customers. Our customers are our lifeblood, without which all the best manufacturing practices in the world are useless. It does not matter if we have the best products in the market, at the best prices, if we have no one willing to buy them. So it makes sense that we need to invest the effort to include customer management in our best practices suite.

Most product manufacturers do not conduct business in isolation. Most, if not all, companies have marketplace competition in their respective industries. With so many choices available to our customer base, how can we make our company and its products stand out from the rest? We need to formulate a customer service *philosophy* to obtain, maintain, and grow market share.

The word *philosophy* is more correct than *plan* in this case. Yes, we will need to develop a *plan* to track customer information. Our plan may include the purchase of some service or system designed to gather customer data. So, whereas gathering and tracking customer data will be necessary at some point, we must first develop our *philosophy* about customers and customer management. A company's philosophy is its mindset, that hidden, nebulous attitude of conducting its business. A philosophy does not easily lend itself to incorporation into a system.

A company's philosophy of *customer service* translates directly into *customer experience*. Customer experience is that impression, feeling, or attitude resulting from the interaction of your customer with someone within your company. What we are striving for is a customer experience that is both consistent and of high quality. Therefore it is vital that we, as a company, establish a documented customer management policy—a policy created with as much forethought and attention to detail as the products we manufacture, a policy that provides guidelines for customer management taken directly from our philosophy. Once created, anyone with the potential for customer contact, from the executive office to a shop supervisor, must understand and be committed to this policy. How well *everyone* understands and executes this policy creates our company's persona in the marketplace.

There is no blueprint to show us how to create a philosophy, and no specification for building good customer relations. Our philosophy draws upon several universal ideas taken from our own personal experiences as a customer. Good customer service means treating our customers as we would expect to be treated as customers ourselves.

Many of the best practices in this book are based on new, modern ways of thinking. Modern manufacturing technologies have evolved at an exponential rate. But people, as it turns out, have not kept evolutionary pace with technology. All people, especially the people who are customers, respond better to the human touch and being treated with respect and courtesy. In the case of customer service, some *old school* principles are still the best approach.

THE START OF A BEAUTIFUL RELATIONSHIP

Managing your customers is not simply a series of business transactions. We build and nurture a relationship with the people who buy our products. This relationship may be as fleeting as a single sale or a long-term commitment spanning many years. As in any relationship there are building blocks that form the foundation upon which all else is built. These foundational elements function to both obtain new customers and help us retain old ones. A great amount of energy is required to keep a good customer relationship alive. Greater effort still is required to find, court, and win a new customer's trust. The best practices customer philosophy therefore centers around these core ideas:

- Accessibility
- Contacts
- Availability
- Responsiveness
- Follow-up
- Customer care
- Customer satisfaction
- Customer recruitment and retention

ACCESSIBILITY

Today, more than ever, technology provides us many different ways to be accessible to our customers. In addition to the simple phone calls and faxes, we now have websites, smart phones, and portable computers to keep us connected. Communication is key to customer satisfaction. Customer service has moved out of the office and now travels with us.

There is nothing more frustrating for a customer than failure to reach someone to address an issue or answer a question. Business offices today rely heavily on automated telephone answering systems and their maze of *Press 1 for sales, Press 2 for technical support*, and so on. While automated phone systems do improve efficiency, it is an improvement focused in the wrong direction. Systems such as these tell your customers that your company's time is more important than their own. A customer calling your company does not want to navigate through long, tedious menu options. She simply wants to talk with someone and resolve her issue *quickly*.

During normal business hours, consider replacing your automated office phone attendant with a real human being, someone who can ask a customer questions and direct the call to the proper person or department. Live interaction with a human being is more efficient at getting your customers to the right place on the very first attempt. It tells your customers that their call is important to you. Live attendants can also advise customers if someone is not available due to vacation or a meeting. Up-front information like this prevents your customers from navigating your entire phone menu only to find their contact is not in the office.

If you use an office-based phone system that has voicemail, please remember to check it often. Be sure to update your outgoing message to reflect your status. If you are out of the office, take the time to change your greeting so your customer knows you are not there. If you use a cell phone, state the cell number on your voicemail greeting to provide an alternative for your customer. Never leave your customer to wonder where you are.

If your company utilizes a website for customer inquiries, review your page design for user friendliness. The link for the *Contact Us* page should be prominently placed on the page, and not buried at the bottom using a tiny font. Give your customers choices to route their issue instead of one generic, catchall form. As a customer, nothing makes me more uncertain of getting a response than seeing a generic e-mail address on a website. I always wonder how long it will take to route all those e-mails to the proper people for resolution.

Without human contact, inquiries via a web page always leave a customer wondering what happens next. Always provide your customer feedback on the anticipated response time. State your response time policy clearly on your contact page or send an automated e-mail showing receipt of the inquiry and expected response date. Use of statements such as, "All inquiries will be answered within two business days from receipt" keeps your customer informed and engaged.

CONTACTS

We have provided the means for customers to contact us. We are accessible and customer inquiries begin. How the inquiry is routed internally for resolution is the next critical step. In large companies, simply connecting the customer to the right internal contact can be difficult. In established relationships, our customer will already have an internal contact. Typically customers will want to talk with their counterparts in your organization. Purchasing talks to purchasing; quality control to quality control, and so forth. For new inquiries and direct consumer contact, however, we need to provide more assistance.

As consumers ourselves we all know the frustration of being bounced from representative to representative within an organization until we find someone to help us with our issue. This is easily avoided by good design work and thoughtfulness when creating your contact systems.

Create standardized lists of questions for live phone help. Create web pages with an extensive FAQ list built and updated by actual inquiries. The idea here is to help your customers better define their issue through leading questions or web options. The better defined the issue, the more likely we can have first-time success in connecting our customers with someone who can help them.

AVAILABILITY

While availability may seem like a reiteration of accessibility, they are entirely different. You can have the latest technology to keep your employees and customers connected. You may have the very best website and contact page, but if your customer representative is never available for interaction, the accessibility options are a moot point.

Nothing is more frustrating to customers than *never* getting directly through to the person they are trying to reach. There is nothing more bothersome for customers than to make contact multiple times before someone addresses their concern. Never make a customer call twice!

As managers we must ensure the employees who are customer representatives are not so overburdened by other internal tasks that customer service becomes secondary. The answer here is staffing an adequate number of people in contact positions to ensure someone is always available to take a customer's call.

RESPONSIVENESS

At this point we have provided means for our customer to contact us with various access methods. We have adequately staffed our organization to guarantee someone is always available to address a customer issue. All this work thus far has merely been to allow contact between ourselves and our customer. The concept of *responsiveness* is the third piece of our customer service philosophy and is the most important of all.

How quickly we can answer a customer's question or how fast we can solve a problem is what really creates customer satisfaction and builds our marketplace reputation. A reputation for fast response can elevate your organization above your competition. We achieve the best customer response with methods that while simple in their concept are often difficult in practice.

Most manufacturers selling direct to consumers are organized to have a dedicated staff whose sole purpose is customer support. This is the ultimate solution for accessibility, availability, and responsiveness. Obviously, your customer support team must be trained in all aspects of your product line, but more importantly, your representatives must have extensive training in conflict resolution and customer psychology. Often, in a consumer situation, a customer calls when there is a problem and the customer is upset. The goal here is to manage a customer's issue without your representative becoming emotionally involved in the discussion. In addition to training, the selection criteria for employees to staff your customer service area must be carefully thought out. It is a given fact that some people have a natural talent for conflict resolution. The hiring process for customer contact positions should include screening tools to identify these individuals.

Then there are manufacturers whose customers are other manufacturers. All manufacturers are a part of the long chain of businesses working to create a final product. In cases such as these, there may not necessarily be a formalized customer support department or help desk. Contact and interactions between two manufacturers often take place between various functional areas within your organization and are rarely routed through a single contact point. The lack of any formalized routing or single point of contact requires us to structure our customer service philosophy differently. In this setting, everyone within your organization can potentially be called to serve as a customer service representative. We need to create a philosophy and policies to guide our employees in the fulfillment of this role in order to reduce response time.

The core concept for the manufacturer-to-manufacturer customer inquiry is this: A customer issue has precedence over *any* meeting, *any* event, or *any* task. Everyone in your organization must be empowered to excuse themselves from any task at hand to assist a customer. It must be understood that assisting a customer shall, and always will, be the *first priority* even if that assistance entails delaying work on an internal request from a C-level manager. This *customer-is-primary* rule must be embraced by the entire organization and the empowerment must flow down from the executive suite to all levels of the organization. Empowerment through the *customer-is-primary* philosophy unleashes the resources of your entire organization, if needed, to find the best answer in the shortest time.

Not all inquiries can be answered in a single day or during the initial contact. Situations are often complex and will require time for thorough investigation. Inform your customers that their situation is going to require more extensive research in order to provide the best answer. Most importantly, tell your customers you plan to provide periodic updates on the status of their inquiry, and then *be sure to do so*. It has been my experience that customers are more patient when kept in the loop regarding your progress with their issue. These status updates also show your commitment to your customer and dedication to your relationship. Commitment and dedication makes for a solid relationship.

Exceptional customer service is a value-added exercise that creates exceptional customer confidence. We demonstrate this philosophy with our eagerness to resolve issues and when we overtly place our customer's needs before our own. Our customers' confidence in our ability to handle their issues will direct new business opportunities to our organization despite product price. As cited in the opening example, people are willing to pay a bit more for a product that has robust customer support.

FOLLOW-UP

Despite our best efforts to resolve a customer issue or answer a question, sometimes we will miss the mark. Never assume that no news is good news because your customer has not given you feedback on your resolution. After a short time, take the initiative to contact your customers to follow up and verify that their situation or question is truly resolved. *Why go looking for trouble?* is an understandable kneejerk reaction to the idea of follow-up initiation. If our customer is quiet, why reopen an issue? To reiterate, the whole idea is to build relationships. We desire to demonstrate our commitment to build a partnership with our customer that is mutually beneficial—a partnership where our customer feels supported and satisfied. Follow-up, therefore, is an essential element in this building process, requires very little effort, and pays for itself by strengthening these relationships that guarantee us future business.

CUSTOMER CARE

The previous section, "Follow-up," delved into the area of building partnerships with our customers. I would like to elaborate on this just a bit more. Customer care is those actions taken by you that lie outside the realm of regular business transactions or problem solving. Customer care involves nothing more than polishing your current customer philosophy. We have all heard it said, "Don't sweat the small stuff." But I believe it is the small stuff that makes us stand out from our competitors. Remember this: The difference between *good* and *excellent* is very small. It is the small efforts that speak volumes to our customers.

Once again, let us look at examples from the manufacturer-to-manufacturer as well as the direct-to-consumer market:

- **"Y'all come see us!"** I love this old Southern expression. It is said whenever someone is leaving after a visit. It means you are welcome back any time and make it soon. Visiting has always been a cornerstone of life in the South, a time for catching up with friends and family, a time to strengthen relationships. In the business world, we can take a lesson from this old and wise tradition. Nothing can better express your commitment to your customers and their satisfaction than taking the time to stop by for a face-to-face visit. The idea of calling on your customers is valid for manufacturer-to-manufacturer and/or businesses selling your product to the direct consumer market. Therefore, if you, or one of your team, happen to find yourselves in an area close to one of your customers, call him up and arrange a cordial visit. Have a meal and take time away from the office to simply talk to your customer about how things are going. While I cannot give you an algorithm to calculate the return on investment for these visits, the positive feeling left with your customer translates to your bottom line. So if you have time and can afford it, "Come see us!"

- **The heavy hitters.** While every single customer deserves our very best care, most manufacturers will have a few customers who represent the majority of their revenue stream. These major customers may require more regular and consistent care. If necessary, and affordable, having an onsite or local representative from your company working within your customer's facility shows an ultimate commitment to your customer's success. These onsite employees are typically well versed in your manufacturing methods, quality control procedures, and technical aspects of your products. Being onsite allows these representatives to quickly address issues as they arise, providing instantaneous feedback and customer support. Onsite support also provides us with a liaison and interpreter. By working in our customer's facility, our representative learns the technical terminology and processing issues faced daily on the customer's shop floor. In doing so, our representative can easily translate and describe customer issues into the industry-specific words we can understand. This translation is invaluable in tracking down root causes for issues by ensuring we fully understand the customer's concerns. Onsite care is the ultimate form of customer service.

■ **John Q. Public.** Manufacturing for direct sales to consumers has many more opportunities for customer care because our consumer base is much larger and more diverse than manufacturer-to-manufacturer. There are so many products competing for our customers' money we must be creative in order to attract and keep their business.

We are all consumers. We all buy things. We want to be treated fairly when spending our hard-earned dollars and we know what attracts us to one product versus another. We also want to know there is support available in the event of a product issue. These ideas are basic and should be common practice across all industries. The basics are *not* what I am talking about here. Customer care at the consumer level is about setting a higher standard than the basics. It is about the entire purchase experience before and after the sale.

■ Not long ago, a co-worker shared a story with me that exemplifies this idea.

My co-worker, whom I'll call Mr. B, was shopping for a new car. After making the rounds to all the local dealers, he was dissatisfied. His experiences ranged from dealer apathy, "Take it or leave it," to arrogance, "You don't want that car, how about this one?" Quotes took forever to get, often involving multiple discussions between dealers and managers. The final list of prices was all over the place for the same vehicle.

In his frustration he called an out-of-town dealer to inquire if they had a car in stock with all the features he wanted and indeed they did. So Mr. B arranged to go check out the car at this one last dealer. The first thing he noticed upon arrival was that the car in which he was interested was freshly washed, detailed, gassed up, and sitting outside the showroom. Mr. B was greeted and warmly welcomed by the manager, who said, "It's all ready for you to take it for a spin," which Mr. B proceeded to do.

The deal was struck and at a price lower than all the other dealers. Now here's where the dealer shows true customer care. During all this time, Mr. B had a son very ill in the hospital. So in addition to the hassle of car buying, Mr. B was also concerned about his son. Mr. B mentioned to the dealer that his son would be excited to see the new car when he was released from the hospital. The dealer asked, "What room is he in?" So Mr. B told him the room number and the dealer responded, "I know where the parking lot is for that section of the hospital. I'll drive you and the car to the hospital and park it where he can see it from his window," and proceeded to do just that.

Needless to say my co-worker became a loyal patron of this dealer for many years. Mr. B's experience of customer care sealed this deal and many more like it. This is a *true story* and reflects how just a small extra effort can pay off for both manufacturer and customer. If you are still not convinced, Mr. B told me that on his next trip back to the dealership, he happened to notice a large sign showing the ranking of all dealerships in the state. This dealer was voted number one in all regards including customer satisfaction. Curiously enough, all the other dealers Mr. B had hassled with earlier were ranked well below the number-one spot. Seems that my co-worker's customer care experience was recognized not only by him but overall by the dealer's industry.

CUSTOMER SATISFACTION

So, how well is your customer philosophy working? Are your customers happy, satisfied, and wanting to do business with you again? Do you know your reputation in the marketplace? Many manufacturers do a decent job at building customer relationships, but fail to take steps to quantify exactly how well their philosophy works. Without implementing methods to gather feedback you are missing out on opportunities to grow, change, and fine tune your philosophy. The feedback method varies depending on your product and customer base, but consider some of the following:

- **After-the-sale follow-up.** This method is very effective in the retail area for big-ticket purchases. Call or e-mail your customers and ask about their overall experience of doing business with you. Keep it short; tell your customers you are contacting them to follow up on their recent purchase and then ask only one question, "What would you change, if anything, about your recent buying experience?" Then listen and let them tell you. Allowing your customers to freely speak their mind will give you far more information than rating scales or closed-end survey questions. Create a log of these comments that can be easily reviewed and analyzed for trends.

- **Track buying habits.** Satisfied customers become repeat customers. Tracking your customers' buying habits is another method to determine customer satisfaction. How many times have they purchased from you and how often? How much do they spend when they make a purchase? Are they buying the same or different products? If all your transactions are single events, perhaps the product itself, or the purchase experience, is not what your customers expected.

- **Returns/complaints.** Do you know the return rate of your products? Can you identify the reason for a product return? Do you retain and analyze customer complaint data? It is obvious that an item is returned, or a complaint registered, when the experience of product ownership was not what your customer desired. Review of return and complaint information can help you uncover and correct product design flaws, performance issues, or weak customer service procedures. Analysis of return and complaint data gives you the feedback to fine tune your product and organization, leading to improvement in your customer's experience of ownership.

Ultimately, gauging customer satisfaction objectively is difficult due to the subjective nature of the data. There will be many different opinions on what the data is telling you depending on who is asked in your organization. Therefore, I recommend that customer satisfaction information be regularly reviewed, in a joint session, with representatives from each functional group within your organization. These multiple viewpoints illuminate the data from all possible angles, offering your organization the best chance at creating a balanced scorecard. Results from these joint reviews should then become action items to be implemented. In turn, the implemented action items should be reviewed for effectiveness at the next joint session. This cycle of collection, review, and correction, when properly done, will guarantee improvement in your customer satisfaction scores, fewer returns, greater market share, and ultimately more profit.

CUSTOMER RECRUITMENT AND RETENTION

Here we have the ultimate goal of our new philosophy: the desire to attract new customers while at the same time strengthening the relationships we have with our established customers. A philosophy that is well planned and consistently applied creates the face we present to the marketplace. Our attitude toward customer care builds our reputation. Rest assured, inconsistent customer service is a death wish for any business.

We gain new market share as much by word of mouth as through all the advertising dollars spent. The amount of new business we earn is directly related to how much effort we put into our customer care philosophy. Think about your own personal experience as a consumer. When you are shopping for your latest new toy, part of your search involves deciding which brand you're going to choose and where you will buy it. But these decisions are only the beginning.

Most likely your research will expand to include store return policies, manufacturer's warranty information, product quality, and the purchase experience. Your research will tap various sources of information. Newspaper articles, trade magazines, websites, and online forums cover the range of information about a company, its customer service, and attitude—information that comes largely from customers themselves. So it is vital that we maintain good relationships with our existing customer base in order to attract new business.

Only after having a complete picture of product and manufacturer will price figure into your decision. Then from our own personal experiences we know that *reputation carries as much weight as price*. Why, then, should we not carry this same understanding forward into our own manufacturing operations? Policies that allow us to be known for both consistently unsurpassed service and high-quality product will indeed attract the new customers we desire and guarantee we hold onto those customers whose trust we worked so hard to gain.

FINAL THOUGHTS

We have learned that our attitude or philosophy toward our customer base, be it retail or otherwise, is foundational to our success and continued growth. Honesty, integrity, and a genuine desire to provide the best purchase experience possible fuel our reputation—a reputation that often is the only difference between us and our competition. Remember these core ideas:

- Make it easy to get in touch with your organization.
- Provide the right people to address your customer's needs.
- Be sure someone is *always available* to address customer issues.
- Customer issues are the first priority.
- Provide constant and consistent communication between you and your customer.
- Follow up to ensure issues are resolved satisfactorily.
- Take care of your customer after the sale.
- Test for customer satisfaction and use the information to continuously challenge your philosophy.
- Hold your reputation sacred.
- Strive to constantly improve your customer's purchasing experience in order to attract new and retain old business.

CHAPTER **11**

Physical Facilities

I once knew a man named Bill who worked as an inspector for a textile company that made high-end fabrics that were sold to manufacturers of uniforms for the military. The last manufacturing step was a finishing process where the fabrics were washed, dried, and wound onto spools. The finishing equipment itself consisted of several wash pans where the fabric was dipped and then ascended upward into a vertical dryer about 100 feet high. These dryers were vented by pipes extending through the outside walls. Due to the vast size and open nature of the finishing area, it was neither heated nor air conditioned.

Bill's job was to cover a station at the end of the production line and record any visual defects as the fabric passed by. The list of defects he watched for was pretty standard for textiles—defects such as missing threads, dirt, oil, and waste, for example. On his list, however, there were two defects that I had never seen before. These were bugs and snow-spots. My curiosity got the best of me and I had to know, so I asked him to explain.

He said, "Well, look up at the top of the drying towers and tell me what you see." Looking up I saw large gaps around the vent pipes where they went through the walls. I also saw open holes where previous vents used to be but were no longer there. I literally could see the sky from the shop floor!

Bill said, "So you see, in the summertime the bugs are attracted to the lights inside and fly in through the holes. Some get caught in the process and wind up smashed into the fabric. In the winter, if it snows, the snowflakes drift down onto the dried fabric and leave a water stain. Sometimes the defects get so bad we have to cut them out."

Bill also told me how difficult it was to work in the summer with the intense heat and how he wore a hat and gloves in the winter to stay warm. Not the best or safest working conditions, to be sure. I did understand, however, why the area was not heated and air conditioned. It would be like throwing money through all those holes.

The physical facilities consist of all the buildings, grounds, equipment, and infrastructure required to create your product. Product quality and profitability are directly affected by the condition of the physical surroundings, equipment, and work areas regardless of the size or scale of your manufacturing operations. It does not matter if you are producing products in a million-square-foot manufacturing site or one located in your garage; best practice dictates we review and optimize areas such as equipment health, work flow, safety, and environmental impact, to name a few. Just like all the other best practices in this book, these concepts are the practical application of good common sense. Let's explore these areas in more detail.

MAINTENANCE

Everything that exists has a life span. Whether natural or man-made, everything around us, including ourselves, will break down in time and cease to function optimally. Breakdown is not a matter of *if* but *when* and comes from two sources: equipment wear and equipment neglect. Every second of downtime in a manufacturing operation translates into real dollars we can never recoup. All is not lost, however. There are steps we can take to prolong the life of our equipment, increase the time between failures, and minimize the impact when failure occurs.

Whereas routine maintenance and preventative maintenance seem similar, they are actually different faces of the same coin. Routine maintenance is the efforts taken to keep equipment operation optimized with regular care. Preventative maintenance recognizes, repairs, and replaces worn equipment parts *before* failure occurs. To illustrate the difference, let us draw on the analogy of owning an automobile.

Routine maintenance for your car includes regularly scheduled oil and fluid changes, replacing filters, washing, waxing, and proper tire inflation. Performance of these maintenance items not only prolongs the life of your engine, car body, and tires but positively affects your gas mileage. Routine maintenance costs us in two ways: time and dollars. A small amount of time is invested while you wait for your car to be serviced or while doing the work yourself. During maintenance your car is offline and not available for use for only a short time. Next, there is the actual dollar cost of supplies, parts, and materials. So by investing in routine maintenance your car will give you longer service with less downtime and is more economical to operate—all of which keeps dollars in your pocket.

Most of us do a fairly good job with routine maintenance. It is in the area of preventative maintenance where we usually fall short. Preventative maintenance on your car includes replacement of critical items such as belts, hoses, timing chains, and brakes. The goal is to replace these items *before a failure occurs*. Failure of these critical components can cause severe collateral damage such as destruction of the car's engine, leaving us stranded, or, even worse, can cause a life-threatening accident. The time and expense to repair the damage caused in these cases is on an order of magnitude greater than what is required to conduct the preventative maintenance in the first place. Unlike routine maintenance, repairing damage that is preventable can take our car, or ourselves, offline for extended periods of time. There is also the possibility that the damage cannot be repaired, nor parts replaced.

The reasons for routine and preventative maintenance are exactly the same in our manufacturing operations. Sometimes we do not take the same vigilance with our production equipment as we do with our cars. We resist taking a machine offline as this costs real money in lost productivity. We monitor equipment efficiencies to determine ways to get more output. We extend the time between routine maintenance striving to squeeze every last bit of production out of our existing equipment.

The results of this inaction *will* result in equipment breakdown and lost productivity *anyway*. A catastrophic failure of a critical part could have you down for weeks waiting for parts and conducting repairs. The best practice here is to implement a maintenance schedule and tie this schedule into your manufacturing planning system. The tie-in to your planning system is critical. Plan and schedule a maintenance order exactly the same as a customer order. There should be a *delivery date* and enough time blocked out on the equipment to get the order completed. This scheduling approach makes it less likely that the maintenance will get postponed or ignored because the equipment is so heavily scheduled with product orders. Placing scheduled downtime into your planning schedule not only allows you to perform the necessary maintenance but also gives your planning staff more accurate information when quoting delivery dates to a customer.

The final part of maintenance planning is having the materials and parts on hand when needed. Whether the downtime is scheduled, or is an emergency, not having the parts you need to quickly address the problem lengthens the downtime and significantly raises the cost. Ideally you would keep a complete spare parts replacement inventory for both planned and unexpected situations. Practically speaking, an inventory this extensive may not be financially possible. If you choose to keep limited stock, seek the guidance of your equipment manufacturer or your own historical records to determine which parts are most likely to fail or are the most difficult to obtain quickly. Regardless of whether you choose full or partial inventory, be certain to have procedures in place to replenish parts and materials as they are consumed.

So, how much does routine or preventative maintenance save us? Can we put a dollar value to being this proactive? Not really, for this would be like trying to predict the future. We would be trying to put a price on something that didn't happen. So while we may not know how much we saved through prevention, we can be *absolutely certain* that with proper maintenance, we have optimized our chances of extended, successful uptime—uptime that translates directly to sustainable productivity, on-time deliveries, and satisfied customers.

THE WORK AREA

Depending on the type of items you produce, you may have your manufacturing facilities set up as continuous-line assembly, specialized departments, or work cells. Regardless of your setup there are common key elements that must be examined in order to optimize throughput and product quality. The following elements are based in part on the methodology named *5S* used in the system known as *lean manufacturing* and are combined with a few ideas of my own.

These elements are:

- Organization
- Identification

- Cleanliness and order
- Safety
- Sustainability
- Stewardship

These elements do not stand alone or work independently of each other. On the contrary, these elements dovetail together, supporting each other and overlapping in their functional results. As we explore each of these individual areas, it is likely that other areas will merge into our discussion. That is the nature of this system.

Organization

Organization means different things to different people. There are no standardized measurement tools to determine levels of organization. There is no endpoint where one can say, "Now, I'm organized!" In my personal experience, I have known individuals who consider having everything simply sorted into separate piles of *stuff* being well organized. Others keep work areas so neat you sometimes wonder if anyone works in the area at all!

Organizing work areas in manufacturing first starts with nothing more than simple observation. Watch the flow of employees and materials as they go about their normal daily routine. These are observations that you, by yourself, most likely cannot make. If you are the manager for an area, you are most certainly indoctrinated into the pulse and flow of your own workspace. Your eyes and mind are calibrated to see and interpret the way things are currently. Through no fault of your own, you are blind to the shortcomings, or opportunities for improvement, within your own area. So, whereas the first step to organization is nothing more than simple observation, you will need help from outside your area in order to accomplish this task.

Your observation team should consist of no more than five individuals taken from other areas within your organization. If possible, choose employees whose primary job responsibilities lie completely outside the actual manufacturing environment and who do not directly touch the product or process. Individuals such as clerks, accountants, and purchasing agents bring the freshest set of eyes to your observation team.

Once you have your team assembled, you cannot simply turn them loose on your shop floor. First, your team must be briefed on all departmental protocols for safety, personal protection, and hazardous material exposure. Remember, many of the individuals on the team may have never before been on the shop floor, so safety is our number-one concern.

To be effective the team must conduct its observations as a group. The team should not be split up and sent separate ways. The dynamic exchange of ideas and observations between team members will yield observations that have more depth and detail—observations and recommendations that have been discussed, debated, and well thought out. One team member should be appointed as scribe to keep notes on all findings, observations, and conclusions.

Remember the intent of the team is to help us optimize the organization of our production area. The team should station themselves at strategic locations where the movement of material and shop employees may be watched without interference of the process flow. The team may need to observe the same operation from several vantage points to obtain a complete picture of the process.

So with the team assembled, briefed, and commissioned, what are they supposed to observe? The purpose of the observation is to watch for apparent wasted motion from employees in the performance of their duties and to determine reasonableness of materials handling, placement, and movement. It is certain that a work flow that requires employees to be constantly moving about to operate equipment or retrieve parts and raw materials is a work flow that is unorganized.

The team must understand that manufacturing a product does not happen in a single step but is in fact a series of smaller steps performed in a sequence much like a dance. There is a rhythm and motion to this manufacturing dance and what we are trying to observe is where the choreography is out of synchronization. We desire to see which steps seem to interrupt the process flow. It will be helpful to your team if you provide guidance in seeing these individual steps by providing flow diagrams or written work instructions for the process being evaluated.

Another great tool for your team is a stopwatch. By timing each individual step, the team can quantify its findings. The resultant timing data will also serve as a benchmark for the measurement of improvements suggested by the team.

With these tools in hand, turn your team loose to observe. Be certain to allow sufficient time for evaluation of both individual process steps and the entire process as a whole. Lengthy processes may have long repeat patterns. The team must be allowed sufficient observation time in order to witness several iterations of all the process patterns. The idea is to ensure that the observation is a repeating problem, not an isolated occurrence or fluke. Processes that are very complex or obviously poorly organized may require you to have more than one team observing around the clock.

The resultant observation list will likely contain findings in the form of simple observations, questions, or suggested changes. These would be findings such as:

- Operator must leave his station to silence equipment alarm located 30 feet away then rush back to station before process completes.

- Why are raw materials staged in the warehouse and not next to the equipment in-feed? Requires 10 minutes to replenish raw materials when needed.

- Move all equipment controls to a centralized station located where entire production line is visible and would require only a single operator.

The observations will shed new light on your organizational challenges. Next, using *your* knowledge of the process, prioritize the findings into those you can correct quickly, at the lowest cost and least disruption, and those findings that require more time and resources to address. Remember, every step of the dance we perfect will affect the flow of the entire performance.

Identification

Integral to the idea of organization is the understanding of identification. We become vulnerable to errors, efficiency losses, and operator confusion when our equipment or raw materials are not properly identified. When we must guess what an equipment setting does, or choose between raw materials that look similar, we are asking for trouble.

Identification issues may be surfaced by the use of observational teams just like the one we used for our organizational study. As a matter of fact, you may conduct the identification audit simultaneously with the organizational study.

What we are looking for in this case are any equipment settings, control, or process locations that do not have some physical means of identification. Similarly, we are looking to see any raw materials or product that is not marked or labeled. Here again, having written work instructions in hand helps raise our awareness.

For example, the instruction requires an equipment setting of 100 pounds per square inch on the pressure gauge. Our equipment has five such gauges, all of which look exactly the same. All the gauges are registering at different levels. Our experienced operator tells us, "Oh, the gauge for that instruction is the third one from the left." There is no label or any marking to indicate this connection between instruction and gauge. Our operator *just knows*. Imagine what is possible when one day our operator is out sick and the equipment must be run by a junior employee. An entire batch of product may wind up unusable for the lack of a one-dollar label.

During your evaluation have the team question the purpose of every knob, switch, or lever that is not marked. Any items found that are not critical to the process should also be labeled as such. Leave no doubt or room for question as to any equipment's purpose.

Maintaining raw material and product-in-process identification is more difficult than for equipment and presents a different set of challenges to your audit team. Typically materials and product will be moving around during manufacture and have many opportunities to become orphaned from their identification. Identification is not a simple sign with only a name or number. We must be able to know *with certainty* we are using the correct materials or taking the proper next process step. We can be certain of these two things only if we have systems in place to identify materials and product as to *what they are* and *where they belong*.

Most people think the term *identification* merely defines *what* something is. On the contrary, identification also contains information about that thing's current *state of being*. Take your driver's license for example; this card is a single document that connects your picture with a name. For most people this connection satisfies the idea of identification. There is, however, more information available on your license. Your height, weight, eye and hair color, age, and address are also listed along with any restrictions you may have regarding your driving privileges. This additional information reflects your state of being at the time the license was issued. Therefore, it is all this information, taken together, that creates your complete identification.

The same concepts are true for raw materials and products-in-process in our manufacturing operations. A properly identified item will have the following four characteristics:

1. The item's physical identification, such as part number or batch (*What is it?*).
2. The current status of that item indicating what stage of processing is completed (*state of being*).
3. The two identification components are clearly written and attached directly to the items.
4. Identification must be attached in such a manner as to prevent loss or damage while in process area.

These four criteria should be used by your audit team during their investigation and any discrepancies and recommendations noted in their final report. For an additional example, see Chapter 5, where we examine a scenario of what can happen when product loses its documentation.

Cleanliness and Order

Central to the methods of 5S is the idea of a clean, well-ordered workplace. Cleanliness and order go hand-in-hand with a well-organized work area. Fast-paced, high-volume production areas can become quickly cluttered as employees go about their duties. Making time to tidy up is a low priority. As with any housekeeping endeavor, it is easier to keep an area clean than to get it clean in the first place.

How do we accomplish this? First, upper management must be involved. The management decision to operate in a clean and orderly fashion must then be expressed to all levels of the organization. Next, the entire management team must provide the tools and, more importantly, the *time* for employees to perform these duties. This means *scheduling time* at the end of an employee's workday for cleanup. The objective here is to leave a work area as pristine as possible for the next set of employees.

Management must also take steps to ensure cleanup equipment like brooms or vacuums are available and in good working order and items such as cleaning chemicals are on-hand and replenished when needed. You have a better chance of successfully keeping your areas clean when you make it easy for your employees to do so.

Orderliness is the other side of this coin. I have seen many manufacturing areas that were reasonably clean but so cluttered that merely walking through the area was like navigating through a maze. We must include orderliness as part of our overall cleanup procedures. The old adage, *a place for everything and everything in its place*, is appropriate here. Therefore, the end-of-day cleanup time should include such things as replacing tools in their proper storage areas and clearing traffic areas of anything that may impede product or personnel flow.

More often than not, housekeeping programs like these start with enthusiasm but quickly become forgotten. This is why it is important for managers to follow up regularly to ensure the newly implemented procedures are being followed.

At this point you may be asking yourself how all this bother about housekeeping has anything to do with optimizing your quality, productivity, and profit. After all, I'm telling you to spend money and valuable time to do so. A cluttered manufacturing area is inefficient. Employees who must navigate my aforementioned maze to perform their duties are wasting time and footsteps and you are losing productivity. An area that is not clean increases your risk of contamination of your product. Dirt from equipment or loose debris can find its way into your manufacturing process, causing losses due to quality complaints, customer returns, or downtime from production equipment damage. All of these increase your costs and negatively affect your profitability. Dirty, cluttered work areas are also a serious safety concern. Employees risk injury when they have to walk on slippery floors or step over junk lying about. A workplace-related employee injury can cost you a tremendous amount of money.

Consider the time and money to keep your manufacturing areas clean and orderly as an investment that extends the life of your equipment, aids in your ability to maintain high-quality standards, and protects your most valuable resource: your employees.

Safety

A manufacturing environment can be a very dangerous place. High-speed equipment, hazardous chemicals, and movement of materials offer numerous opportunities for employee injury. Keeping our employees safe *is* our number-one priority. Providing safety procedures and protection to our employees far outweighs any productivity or profitability goals. If we, as management, cannot adopt the attitude of *safety first*, I contend that perhaps we do not need to be managers or in business at all. That sounds rather harsh, doesn't it? This strong statement speaks to the passion that best practices companies must have toward the care and protection of their employees. This passion is more about doing what is right than preventing lost revenue from an employee accident. It is true, the cost of accidents and injuries can quickly add up from medical bills, lost productivity, and possible legal issues. These costs do affect your bottom line. However, no amount of money can begin to compensate an employee for the life changes brought about by a disabling accident.

Not all accidents are avoidable; that is why we call them *accidents*. What we must do is to take every step possible to minimize risks. These steps must be undertaken in a formalized system that combines training, inspections, and education.

Everyone in your company must be involved in the safety program, and overseeing safety cannot be a part-time affair. Whereas safety is every employee's responsibility, management of the safety program cannot be effectively handled by segmentation of responsibilities as an add-on to a manager's other duties. Best practices for safety begin with the appointment of a *dedicated safety director*. This individual's only job is to oversee the *entire* safety program in your company. The safety manager is responsible for the creation, implementation, and oversight of procedures, plans, and protocols to ensure compliance to all local, state, and federal safety laws. The safety manager shall conduct walking audits on the shop floor and is charged with correction of any situation deemed unsafe even if the correction involves the curtailment of production equipment.

Employees move around while doing their daily duties. This may expose them to multiple hazards not found in their home work area. Therefore, the safety manager must ensure that every employee, without exception, receives training in baseline safety protocols for *all* potential safety hazards found in *any* work area. Completion of this basic training is required before *any* new employee is allowed on the shop floor. In addition, everyone should have a refresher course on safety basics on some given frequency. Then there are those employees whose duties have greater risks and require specialized, in-depth training or certification. If such specialized training cannot be conducted in-house, the safety manager is responsible for the arrangement of outside training and keeping certifications up to date.

Listed next are areas of training that should be covered in your basic safety training. While detailed instruction may not necessary in all areas, discussion and exposure to the topics is recommended. Some employees will require more in-depth training in certain areas in order to perform their assigned duties.

Basic safety education should cover:

- Slip and fall hazards
- Back health and lifting techniques
- Pinch points
- Eye protection
- Hearing protection
- Respirator training
- Protective gear, suits, shoes, gloves, and disposal protocols
- Decontamination procedures
- Spill control

- Hazardous materials handling and understanding Material Safety Data Sheets
- Lock-out and tag-out procedures for equipment
- Basic firefighting techniques such as use of fire extinguisher
- Evacuation procedures and routes
- Materials handling equipment such as lifts, cranes, or elevators
- Equipment controls and emergency stops
- Locations of all first-aid equipment, eye wash, and emergency showers
- Understanding all posted signs, labels, and floor markings
- Most importantly: Education in safety awareness and the understanding that the employee has the right and responsibility to stop any work or equipment when a situation is deemed unsafe

As you can see, safety cannot be a simple add-on system living on the margins of your everyday operations. Your employees are counting on you and your management team to provide a workplace where safety is embedded in the very heart of all your systems. By creating such a robust *safety system*, you are in fact creating a *safety culture* that will hopefully provide your company with many, many person-hours without an accident. A safety culture generates more dollars than it spends by preventing employee downtime due to accident. Finally, it is a culture where employees are able to go about their daily jobs without fear of being hurt. This, perhaps, is the greatest benefit of all.

Sustainability

The next in our series of concepts taken from 5S is the idea of sustainability. Although this concept is the easiest to discuss, it is the most difficult to obtain. All the effort we put into organization, identification, cleanliness, and safety is lost if someone does not routinely follow up to ensure all our systems are still in place and utilized. Systems like this are usually embraced with a lot of energy at the start—energy that tends to get redirected as the issues of daily production creep in. Management, therefore, from top level down, must show their commitment to our practices through regular briefings or meetings to review the status of the current system as well as ongoing improvement opportunities. Managers should make audits on the shop floor and have discussions with employees about how well the current practices are performing. We must make the *review of what we do* as important as *doing what we do*.

Stewardship

The final discussion about our physical facilities centers around the idea of stewardship. This may sound out-of-place at first, but remember that as managers we are entrusted with the care of all the grounds, machinery, buildings, and people. Stewardship requires the adoption of a service mentality. We desire to provide the very best environment and work experience possible for our employees.

Stewardship also entails being a good corporate neighbor. Unless your facilities are located on another planet, you are surrounded by the world at large. Be it other manufacturing facilities or residential neighborhoods, your facility has an impact on everyone and everything surrounding it. While there are plenty of local, state, and federal regulations to protect everyone from the impact of your operations, practicing good stewardship goes beyond what these laws require. Take the time to find out who your neighbors are and ask if they have any issues with your facility. Increased traffic, bad smells, noisy equipment, and bright lights at night are all part of the daily life around manufacturing sites. Are any of these causing a problem for your neighbors? Ask, find out, and take action to correct any neighborhood concerns and minimize your impact footprint.

Being a good corporate neighbor also means you take pride in your facilities' outward appearance. If your grounds have grassy or natural areas, are these areas well kept and landscaped? Do your facilities have peeling paint, abandoned buildings, or discarded equipment stored outside in plain sight? Why should this matter? Who cares what the outside looks like, or the inside for that matter? How does this help me make a better-quality product or more profit?

Your facilities' outward appearance and how your present yourself in your neighborhood is a direct reflection on your attention to details. The resulting negative or positive reaction among your neighbors and your customers can result in differences in sales and perception of quality. Put simply, if you were a customer, would you think a company whose facilities looked old and run down would be capable of producing a quality product? If the company can't be bothered with everyday details like appearance, then what makes you think its attention to product details and quality would be any better?

Stewardship extends beyond your local site to the entire globe. Where possible, embrace methods and materials that have less environmental impact on the planet. Research alternative sources for raw materials. Choose to purchase from suppliers who share the idea of reducing environmental impact. Explore alternative or renewable sources of energy. Create programs to reduce the amount of waste you produce and landfill. Start a recycling program for your internal waste. Be creative and determine whether the waste from your manufacturing processes can be reused by another industry. All of these green ideas can affect your bottom line profitability through energy savings, reduced waste removal and landfill costs, and revenue generated through the sale or use of recycled materials.

FINAL THOUGHTS

It may have been hard to imagine that so much internal attention to equipment, organization, safety, and buildings really mattered. Hopefully, you now see that it is an essential part of your goal to optimize and improve. Your physical facility is *home* for yourself and your employees for at least one-third of your day. Let us strive to provide everyone the very best experience possible during this time. The physical presence of your facility is there for everyone to see *every day*. Let us also strive to set a good-neighbor example for everyone around us. You are guaranteed a return on investment by utilizing these best practice techniques to maintain equipment, organize your work areas, and provide a clean, safe environment for your employees and neighbors. This is an investment return that combines less downtime, increased efficiency, employee satisfaction, consistent quality, and industry recognition into a corporate presence attractive to both customers and peers alike—a corporate presence that sets a *new standard* for quality products and customer service that leaves your competition in the starting gate when the race is won.

CHAPTER **12**

People

At various times throughout my professional career I have had opportunity to interact with many of the associates at SAS Institute. During this time I have also been privileged to hear Dr. Jim Goodnight, CEO and co-founder of SAS, speak about his vision for the company, which earned SAS No. 1 on *Fortune* magazine's annual "100 Best Companies to Work For" for 2010. Time and again Dr. Goodnight expresses the importance of people. Both in lecture and print, when asked what his job was at SAS, Dr. Goodnight says, and I paraphrase, "Every day, this company's greatest assets go out the front gate. My job is to see they return."

This is a sentiment I deeply share with Dr. Goodnight. As a young man, I was hired by my present employer in a utility position. My job was to do all the odd jobs that needing doing, including restocking supplies, loading and unloading equipment, and sweeping up. I learned first hand, and from the ground up, what employees want from managers. I understand the desire to get ahead and to be treated fairly. It is more than a paycheck. It is about having a sense of security and of being understood. It is about being recognized foremost as a person. So, our challenge as managers is this: How do we best understand and define the best practices for managing employees?

I've left this chapter until last because it is the most important. All of the previous discussions about best practices are meaningless without people. The men and women of your workforce, from janitor to president, are your single most valuable resource. Without them, all the finest equipment in the world, the latest technologies, and the most complete work instructions are nothing more than piles of metal, plastic, and paper. It is the people, those who make the entire manufacturing process happen, who convert all your efforts into products and company profits. Most definitions of the word *company* read something like this: "a grouping or gathering of people." Without our people, we have no company.

In my humble opinion, and with all due respect to my friends in human resources, our industries lost something when we started using the term *human resources*. In the early years of my employment it was called *personnel*, and I still think this is the better term. What we are dealing with here are living, breathing persons, not another resource like equipment, energy, or raw materials. People have needs, emotions, drives, and desires that elevate them above the term *resource*. People are dynamic with needs that change from minute to minute, day to day, year to year—needs far more diverse and challenging than setting up machinery and allowing it to run.

The term *human resources* creates a barrier and places a distance between ourselves as managers and those who make up our workforce. I believe we created this new term to somehow cushion ourselves psychologically when managing the difficult decisions we often face that go hand-in-hand with managing employees. Admittedly, managing people, especially employees, can be a very messy business.

That being said, we must take a different attitude toward our management style. We must evaluate how we interact with our employees and understand the manager–employee dynamic. Most importantly, we must work hard to understand what our employees expect of us. Here are a few of the basic ideas we should keep in mind.

We are the stewards of our employees and for this reason we are charged with the mission to become the very best stewards possible. Our employees rely on us to make good decisions on their behalf, for our decisions affect their lives and livelihood. Employees expect a degree of reliability and consistency when it comes to our relationship. We should strive to present a degree of stability in our interactions and not let ourselves be carried across the entire spectrum of emotions when dealing with issues. Our employees look to us for guidance in times of trouble and a pat on the back for a job well done. We have to become both counselor and coach. Best practices for managing employees require attention to all the needs of our *personnel*. It means providing an environment that nurtures safety, productivity, stimulation, respect, and personal satisfaction. The end result is this: When a solitary employee experiences personal growth, the entire company grows as a result. It is, therefore, always a benefit to the company to promote an employee's gains.

Much of what I know about managing employees comes from an anthology of sources and exposure to programs like "Zenger Miller—Front Line Leadership," "Myers Briggs," "Maslow's Hierarchy of Needs," and the like, cobbled and held together with the scars from lots of mistakes. This gives me a real working understanding of how employees respond to and interact among one another and with managers. Best practices in this case are personal. They require me to be the very best I can be and to do the very best I can, as a manager, to provide for my employees. I also believe and understand that no employee wakes up and makes the conscious decision, "Today I will do a bad job at work!"

Most problems with employees, such as poor workmanship, spotty attendance, or bad attitude, result from unfulfilled needs. These needs are as diverse as the employees themselves. The more we understand these needs, the better we are as managers in our ability to address them.

EDUCATION

Ed has been on the same job in our company for 35 years. He is the best mechanic we've ever had. Hired at age 21, he was just starting out in life and had a young family to support. Ed had a natural mechanical ability to fix things, picked up from working in his dad's garage as a kid. These naturally acquired skills gave Ed all he needed to begin his life and career. Today, after 35 years, Ed's skills are finely polished but there is a problem. In years past, Ed was merely given verbal requests about what needed fixing and he fixed it. Today, our company issues printed work requests and requires logging in information about the work completed into our computerized system. This new system allows better tracking of time and parts, and gives organization to the requests. This new system also totally cripples our finest mechanic. You see, Ed cannot read.

No one would argue that formal education is a bad thing. Education is the foundation upon which all other knowledge is built. When choosing our employees, it is necessary to require a basic set of skills. Not every person we employ needs a Ph.D. in manufacturing; however, the basics of reading, writing, math, and fluency in the local language are essential. Without these skills, neither our employees nor ourselves have a good chance of success.

The best practice in this case is the development of screening tools, typically tests, that allow our potential new employees the opportunity to demonstrate their abilities. Never take at face value the information on a resume or application. As we know, our education system today is sorely lacking in teaching the basics. Confirmation is only a short test away and should be a part of our hiring process and decisions.

But what about the employees we already have? I mean the ones already a part of our company who may or may not possess the basic skills. Basic skills were not necessarily required back in the day when getting a job meant showing up, maybe filling out a simple application, and going to work. The environment of the workplace and subsequently the requirements for the jobs have grown and changed. Yet, our employees are the same. How do we invest in these dedicated long-term employees who may need a little help to catch up?

One of the most elegant solutions I've come across evolved within my own company many years ago. We knew or suspected that some of our employees read very poorly or not at all. Some had difficulty with simple math. Many did not have the opportunity to finish their primary education simply because they had to go to work to help out their families. Whatever the reason, their jobs now required more and better skills and we needed experienced employees who could adapt. The solution was simple. A notice went out to the bulletin boards throughout the facility that our company would be offering free tutoring in reading and math to anyone who was interested. The classes would be after work, on the employees' own time, and taught by volunteers from within the company. Our volunteer instructors were managers who were former schoolteachers and were actually the ones who started the program. The company set aside classroom space, and provided materials at company expense. The goal was twofold: first, to provide refresher courses for those who had completed primary education but still lacked mastery, and second, to prepare those who did not complete their primary education for taking the GED equivalence exam. The response to this offer was well accepted. Many of our very-long-term employees participated in the program and some went on to receive their GED.

In addition to providing in-house education, we had many employees who desired to further their education at institutes of higher learning. Once again, we made an investment. We set up a program of tuition aid for anyone wishing to enroll in a selected list of area colleges and universities. Students completing a class with a "C" or better average would receive tuition refunds. To date, we have many employees taking advantage of this program.

My company did not have to make these investments. Our managers did not have to donate their time. But they did, because an investment in employees has a guaranteed return. We now have employees who feel the company has their best interest in mind, which is true. The company now has a more educated workforce, who possess a more up-to-date level of skills, and are prepared to use, understand, and participate in modern manufacturing methods.

TRAINING

> Martin was having real problems. It seemed that no matter how hard he tried, the quality of product he produced from our equipment always fell short of the quality produced by his peers. This was understandable when Martin was first hired; after all, there is an expected learning curve. It is now six months later and Martin's performance is no better than before. To the untrained eye, Martin was working very hard, running around constantly adjusting the machine in an attempt to improve the quality. What is not apparent, however, is that Martin was never told there was an exact sequence to the adjustments; nor was he told how long to wait between adjustments to see the true effects on the product. Martin was working very hard, with honest intentions, but in the wrong direction. Martin was the victim of poor training.

Nothing frustrates an employee faster that being unsure of how to accomplish the task at hand. You can create reams of very detailed documents, with instructions on how to do a particular job, but this documentation must be followed up with training. Written instructions and directions are made up of words. I am certain that at some time in your life, you have had your words misinterpreted. Words alone cannot always convey what we are trying to say. When it comes to performing a job-related task, nothing can replace the training of the new employee by one of your more experienced employees. The best practices training system consists of qualified trainers, a training plan, documentation, and follow-up.

The cornerstone of the training system is the trainers themselves. These trainers must be qualified by demonstrating mastery of the job as observed by their managers or independent quality assurance personnel. The qualification is accomplished by use of a documented checklist. This list details all the job elements, skills, quality points, safety practices, and related work instructions. The trainer needs to show proficiency with each item, and management needs to sign off on the trainer as qualified in the particular job skills. The checklist becomes part of the trainer's permanent record.

Next, the trainer must be able to communicate his or her knowledge to the new employee. It does no good to have a qualified trainer who cannot teach. Once a trainer shows proficiency in the job, he or she must next be observed for a while actually training someone. If and when the trainer's skills meet with management approval, then the trainer is fully qualified and his or her record updated accordingly. This update to the trainer's employee record becomes the foundational evidence for your training system and creates an accreditation for the training received by new employees. The qualification record also provides justification for the increased wages some companies pay to trainers.

One word of caution here: Do not assume your most experienced employees are already qualified and you can skip the qualification steps. *Each candidate must be screened.* Just because someone has done the job for years does not mean she is the most proficient or has teaching ability. I once heard someone describe it this way: "The worse-case scenario is to have a really *bad* driver who is a really *good* teacher!" You can imagine the opposite scenario to be possible as well: Great drivers cannot necessarily teach. Either way, the results will not be what you desire.

There remains the question of what happens when a candidate for trainer fails to meet management approval or shows no skills for training. The answer is to be proactive in the candidate interview and selection process. It is vital to have documentation that contains very specific details of the qualification procedures and training skills assessment. These details are covered in depth by the managerial team during the interview process with trainer candidates. In order to avoid confusion, managers must emphasize during the interview that the candidate is being considered based on his or her knowledge and experience and there are no negative repercussions or actions taken if the candidate does not meet management approval. In the event an employee does not meet approval, the record of the attempt is recorded in the employee's permanent record solely to document the event. The employee is also provided feedback regarding the reasons for not being approved. Managers must reiterate that no negative results will come from the attempt. If we have an employee we feel has potential but who cannot meet approval on the first attempt, the best practice strategy is to arrange for additional training for our candidate, in areas deemed deficient, in order to improve his or her chances should another attempt be made.

You may question the necessity of going to all this effort to have qualified trainers. The simple answer is *consistency*. With qualified trainers solely responsible for teaching all your new employees, you get the same teaching every time. Simply teaming up a new hire with just anyone doing the job guarantees your new employees will have as much variation in the skills and understanding as the number of current employees to which they were matched.

The next element of training is the creation of a documented training plan. If you ask several employees who do the same job about the most important skills or knowledge in doing that job, you will get many different answers. As managers, we are charged with putting together a training plan that reflects the best practices for accomplishing a particular job. This becomes a written document, a checklist that can be used by your new employee to navigate through the logical sequence of exercises and training. These checklists are tied to written work instructions that document the procedures in detail. Many companies today are also producing in-house video for use as a training tool and as a supplement to the written instructions. If you have resources to produce and provide video, it is encouraged. The training plan, instructions, and video, taken together with our qualified trainers, are our assurance of complete and consistent training and orientation of our employees.

In developing our work instructions and training plans it is vital to include an in-depth explanation of why each procedure is required. Only when working with robots is no explanation of *why* required. If your trainees understand both what they are doing and why they are doing it, you have a greater chance of first-time success and less confusion or frustration.

Finally, your training system must address two additional items: First, the system must require a review and retraining of former employees who are returning to a job once held after being gone for an extended period. This is necessary in order to refresh their skills and make them aware of any changes since they last performed the job. Second, the system must have provision for review of any changed work instructions to ensure all employees are using the latest procedures.

To complete the training we must follow up with new employees after they have been on the job for a short time. We need to give them enough time to master the tasks at hand, yet follow up early enough to correct any bad habits or misunderstood instructions before they become ingrained. Taken together, a properly implemented, well-designed training system becomes a core element of your best practices suite.

MENTORING

Robert works as a lab technician in our quality control area and has been in his current position for about five years. The lab manager, Mike, has always been impressed with Robert's ability at problem-solving when a quality issue arises that is not covered by a written procedure. Robert's logical thinking and solutions have turned into new procedures on many occasions and prevented countless errors and off-quality product. Mike understands that Robert has a mind and a talent for quality control. Rarely in Mike's 25 years as lab manager has he come across such talent. Therefore, Mike gives Robert the more challenging tasks, often those related to testing for new product development. Of course, Robert excels with these new projects, and Mike makes sure Robert receives the well-deserved credit. In two years, Mike moves on to retirement; Robert is promoted to lab manager.

We occasionally hear the terms *mentoring* or *apprenticeship* as it relates to skilled trades, but true mentoring is seldom seen in today's industrial environment. Mentoring is different from training in that mentoring instills a philosophy or way of thinking. It tackles problem solving and ethics and shows how our manufacturing systems interrelate. Mentoring moves away from the particular job skills to the higher, global view. From this vantage point, a junior employee can see past just the job at hand to the bigger company objectives, understand how processes interrelate, and prepare for the next level in his career.

Mentoring typically happens outside any formalized system. If we are lucky, we will have a few senior employees who see untapped potential in one of the new junior employees. These seniors will then take it upon themselves to bring out the junior's unexpressed skills and talents.

This process can have tremendous impact for your company for it allows an inheritance of information, skills, and best practices. While mentoring can be set up as a formal program, I do not believe it needs to be for day-to-day operations. As managers, I believe best practice demands we simply create the environment to nurture this behavior. First, we must instill a sense of freedom to mentor into our senior staff. We must let them know that our company is open to the idea of grooming fresh talent. We should listen to our seniors when they point out new employees with potential talents. We should find job situations where juniors and seniors can mix and interact. Put both on the same team to accomplish a task. Create a learning environment. This should be sufficient to allow natural teaching to occur. Those seniors with the skills and desire to teach will do so and feel recognized for their vast experience. Those juniors with the ambition and desire will migrate to their mentors.

There is only one situation where I believe a more formalized approach is needed. Most companies are well aware that all of their more senior employees will be retiring at a future date. As these seniors move closer to that time, we as managers need to prepare others to fill their role. They cannot be truly replaced, only represented, but someone must be waiting in the wings. The biggest mistake companies make is letting decades of knowledge simply walk out the door. Our best hope of minimizing the damage in these cases is to formally create the mentor and apprentice roles. The key to success with this idea is timing. We cannot suddenly realize that our senior is retiring in six months and drop in a potential replacement candidate at that time. Our candidate cannot possibly absorb decades of experience in six months. This overloading will merely cause the candidate frustration and anxiety, and possibly kill his motivation.

If we know we have an invaluable senior within a few years of leaving, we should create the apprenticeship *now* to allow the maximum amount of time for the training. As previously mentioned, employees being informally mentored become our source for this more formal in-depth grooming. We must also solicit the assistance of our retiring senior in the selection process for the replacement. This creates a vested interest within the senior, gives the senior a feeling of control, and helps promote his understanding that he isn't being kicked out of the door to make room for new employees.

By whatever method you choose, mentoring provides a way to retain some of their wisdom and experience when our best employees move on to the next phase of their lives, which makes this a must-have best practice.

EMPOWERMENT

Let's meet a hypothetical employee we'll call Mary. Mary has been with our company for 15 years and is a lead operator on our manufacturing floor. Mary has had some higher education beyond high school, has received extensive cross training on all the jobs within her department, and works closely with the company's engineering team on new product development. As her manager, I know Mary does not need constant supervision and merely requires a request from me and the freedom to take the ball and run with it. I have specifically commented to Mary that I consider her responsible for her department and the product she produces. This says, "I trust you." Mary is empowered in her job because she feels both in control and responsible for her part of our business. I have few, if any, work-related issues with Mary. Simply put, Mary knows what she is doing and I let her do it. This makes Mary not just an employee, but in a sense, a partner in our business.

It has been often said that *knowledge is power*. Knowledge is the accumulation of education, training, mentoring, and experience. Knowledge is also *empowering*. When employees feel empowered they are not as likely to have as many problems in the workplace.

Employees can sometimes feel powerless when working in a strictly regulated workplace. Although it is wise to manage your business with best practices, we must also take care that those same practices do not strip our employees of their sense of purpose and investment in the business. Empowerment means giving not only the responsibility for the job but the authority to act when the need arises. The stress of responsibility without the authority to take action hamstrings our employees, creates a sense of powerlessness, and leads eventually to apathy. We empower our employees by setting up guidelines within the scope of our process controls that allow them the freedom to make critical decisions while on the job.

As managers, we have to relinquish the idea of total control and let our employees do what they do best. If we've carefully trained our employees, provided clear process instructions and information, and placed the best candidates in the job, there is no reason to micromanage. Employees work best when they have a complete sense of ownership in their daily activities. Empowerment also allows our employees to challenge current practice when they find a better way to perform a task. The fear of retaliation is gone because empowered employees feel they are working in conjunction with, and not against, management.

The benefits are obvious. We have employees who feel appreciated, whose opinions count, thus creating a more stable workforce that is willing to team with management to provide a quality product. Again this boils down to communication with our employees. We need to ask them if they have issues or suggestions about their workplace or job. This can be face to face or by surveys if your organization is larger. The method is not important; *the asking is*. However, asking is not enough; we must take action to correct situations when we can and be ready to offer reasonable explanations when we cannot. This is the only way we have to let our employees know that their opinion counts. Our actions speak louder than our words, and our responses empower our employees. Empowered employees then become the supporting structure for our entire organization and a benefit to the entire company.

EMPLOYEE BENEFITS

> Tom came to the company about three years ago fresh out of college and ready to start his life. His position as salesman required extensive global travel and a lot of time on the road. Very quickly, Tom became a star in the sales force, bringing in new business and revenue like no one before him. Recently, Tom was happy when he married his college sweetheart and they had their first child. Tom and his new wife also faced a challenge. Tom's newborn son was born with serious health issues that required extensive hospital stays and created large hospital bills. Therefore, Tom needed to stay closer to home to assist with their son. There was no provision in the company's policies for working from home. Tom was denied that option. As time progressed, Tom's son exceeded the small maximum limit allowed by the company's insurance plan and the bills really started to pile up. Tom was rapidly running out of options, so he turned to the one thing he knew best. Tom used his talent for sales to sell himself to a new company, one that was forward thinking and flexible enough to provide for Tom and his family the benefits they needed to carry on with their lives.

Let's be honest. Most of us work every day to support the lifestyle to which we are accustomed. No one, except a very few, work just for the joy of working. There are benefits to be had: money, security for both ourselves and our family's future, health care, recognition of our efforts, and the opportunity to learn and grow. Unfortunately, in today's economic environment, benefits are usually the first on the chopping block when our company decides to conserve financial resources. Our employees depend upon us for the livelihood of their families and themselves. They expect more than just a paycheck in return for their time. Therefore, when it comes to employees, having an attractive benefits package is definitely the best practice.

Today's young talented people move around more, changing jobs far more often than I did when I started my career. Today's talent is not afraid to leave a company in search of another with better benefits, pay, and growth opportunities. When we lose someone for these reasons, we've lost our entire investment in that person. We are left back at square one and must now find a replacement. All our efforts of training, education, and most importantly, experience, walk right out the door. So our efforts are best spent in keeping the employees we have. It is less expensive to keep them than to replace them.

Before we go any further, let me say this. Structuring a benefit plan that fits your company's needs must be tailored by you. Only you and your company management have the knowledge and ability to create and implement such a package. No book, anywhere, can give you the specifics on what will work best for you or how to do it. There are, however, core benefit concepts that have proven themselves successful time and again. It is from this 40,000-foot level that we approach this idea of *benefits*.

Financial

Salary or wages is a good starting point. Compensation must be competitive with the market as a whole, not just regionally. The skilled workforce today is willing to move to where the better jobs are located. So we are, in essence, competing on a national, if not global, level for their abilities. There are many resources available through human resources groups and on the Internet that compile salary information for job types, descriptions, and locations. Careful study of this information is essential in making sound decisions regarding salary scales. There also must be a sound, structured policy for determination of raises, bonuses, and commissions that is transparent, understandable, and fairly administrated.

Profit sharing is another way to supplement salary and boost employee morale. It brings a cohesiveness to your employees by giving them a common goal. When the company is successful, they share in that success. Typical profit-sharing programs are paid annually and are a percentage of gross salary.

Everyone desires to have financial security for our later years when we leave the workforce to enjoy retirement. Whereas many companies today leave retirement planning to the individual, I believe it is in everyone's best interest, and the best practice, to offer our employees assistance to assure their golden years.

There are many individual plans available today and we should assist our employees with their retirement decisions by offering information and education about retirement planning. If your company can afford to do so, a company-sponsored retirement plan is an excellent idea. An ideal company plan includes contribution matching. Contribution matching is when the company matches the employee's contribution to the retirement plan, dollar-for-dollar. The company match ratio increases, over time, based on the employee's age. Contribution matching gives a real incentive to employees who may otherwise never participate in a plan. If you do choose to offer profit sharing, you can offer your employees the option to contribute all or part of this money into the retirement system as well.

Health Care

Health care is a benefit getting lots of attention today. With the high cost of medical care, offering a comprehensive health-care package is a sure way of attracting the brightest and best talent. This benefit should cover not only doctor and hospital care, but pharmacy, dental, vision, and prevention.

One of the more attractive additions to this benefit is preventative care. It is far cheaper to invest in the health of your workforce than to treat the illness and disease. The preventative benefit includes annual physicals, screening tools like mammograms, and blood analysis. You may consider having an in-house nurse practitioner so your employees can be seen for minor problems or get a prescription without their having to miss large amounts of time from work and the company having to absorb the cost of a doctor visit. An on-site practitioner can have a dramatic effect on keeping insurance costs down. Prevention also includes wellness programs. You may consider offering in-house classes on nutrition and fitness. Organizations like Weight Watchers and Take Off Pounds Sensibly (TOPS) offer assistance in corporate programs. Offer smoking-cessation programs that cover the entire cost of medications and assistance in quitting. You can set aside a small space to create an in-house fitness room with equipment for cardiovascular workouts and weightlifting machine stations. My current employer hires a fitness trainer once a week to guide our employees in group workout activities. These sessions not only provide physical health benefits but create a sense of camaraderie among co-workers. Remember that keeping your employees healthy helps them stay productive and on the job. Whether attracting younger, more health-conscious employees or helping your current staff stay well, a comprehensive health-care benefit is an essential best practice.

Vacation

Even your very brightest or most experienced employees will most often push themselves too hard. Today's fast-paced work environment often calls for putting in more hours in a week than did our parents. We also have the new burden of always being connected. Smart phones, texting, e-mail, and voicemail are all ways to be sure we are never really off the job. These tools make us more productive but also prevent us from pulling the plug to rest and unwind. A benefit we cannot ignore is vacation time. While the amount of time allowed is a company decision, there should be sufficient time given to allow employees to truly be away from the job stress. I advocate starting new employees with a minimum of one week, adding one day for each year served after that. A cap of total days is up to you. You must also have some incentive for your employees to actually take advantage of this benefit, such as limiting the number of days you may carry over from one year to the next. Rules such as this force your employees to take the beneficial time off or risk losing it. Finally, allow your employees to take vacation time in small increments, say one-half day at a time. Often just having the afternoon off can make a world of difference.

As a manager, it is up to you to be sensitive to the state of your employees' needs for time off. Increased mistakes, bad attitude, and increased sick days are all signs that your employees may need time away. Frank and honest discussion with your employees about taking time off should be a part of your overall management plan. Let them know that it is okay for them to be away. As managers we need to structure our company so this is true. No company should be so dependent on a single individual that its operation is compromised by that individual's absence. Tell your employees that when they are on vacation, they are not to *check in* just to be sure. When you're on vacation, you are on vacation.

You must remember that managers are employees too, and as such should play by the same rules. When we are away, we should make provisions with our management team to ensure coverage during our absence so we are not compelled to stay in touch. Most managers do not model this behavior. Managers who check and respond to e-mail, voicemail, or text messages while on their own vacations undermine the idea of being unplugged and set a different expectation within the company. Simple planning can allow both yourself and your employees to enjoy the benefits from well-deserved downtime.

Children and Family

For our employees with children, we must understand that those little ones come first in our employee's lives. Taking care of a sick child, getting to a doctor's appointment, and meetings for school usually happen during working hours. How we set the rules for this time away is up to us. The important aspect is to ensure that our employees know we are aware of their situation and have made allowances in our rules, within reasonable limits, to accommodate them. In today's world, usually both parents are working. There are also many single-parent homes as well. Care for the children, especially preschoolers, becomes a real issue of time and money. Really progressive companies realize that the time and expense of daycare can put a financial and psychological drain on its employees and that an employee concerned about his or her child's welfare is not focused on the tasks at hand. So many companies are offering in-house, company-sponsored daycare. Usually this comes at a reduced employee cost, allows closer interaction between a parent and child, and makes for a much healthier experience for both.

Despite our best efforts, life is life, and events occur that simply must be dealt with. Illness, whether personal or a loved one's, children, and sadly, death are a part of employees' lives. We must make allowances in our management strategies and benefit plans to support our employees at these times. We should have in place a method of sick leave that allows significant time off for employees dealing with illnesses. Sick leave may be with reduced pay depending on the company's ability to compensate. We should also include paid time off for a few days to handle all the issues and events surrounding the death of a close family member. We must understand that employees have extended families, families that exist outside the societal norm of the traditional. These are people not related by blood or marriage, such as lifelong friends or significant others. Nonetheless, these extended family members are also a vital part of our employee's life and, as such, cannot be treated any differently than *traditional* family. Our employees will need to deal with exactly the same issues with their extended family as the traditional one. Consider extending benefits such as health care and medical screenings to domestic partners in your benefits package. We should, therefore, think of all the people in our employee's life as *family* and make allowances accordingly.

Remember, we are not just hiring a single person. We are establishing a link between two families; our total workforce *family* and all the people who are a part of an individual employee's life.

Here are a few parting thoughts on benefits. Manufacturing today does not always mean all your employees are on the factory floor. They may work together but not in the same physical location. Processes may be scattered around the globe. Employees may interact with each other daily but never meet face to face. Your employees come from many cultures, lifestyles, and countries.

The benefit package elements mentioned cover the basics and have been around for a while. Although we would agree that most of these benefits are simply the right thing to do, many of these benefits are dictated to us by law. This is because at some point in history, employers did not always do *the right thing*.

Depending on how progressive your company is, you may wish to offer additional benefits that are outside the scope of the traditional that acknowledge this new environment and embrace the idea of *doing the right thing*. These additional benefits include telecommuting, flextime, and antidiscrimination policies for minority groups not yet included by a federal mandate.

Allow telecommuting for employees whose physical presence is not needed daily. They may satisfy their duties via an online presence while working from home. Telecommuting is a real help to employees with children or who live a longer distance from the workplace. Telecommuting saves money on child care and transportation costs, and removes vehicles from the road, making it a green alternative.

If your company operates its manufacturing around the clock, offering alternative schedules is appealing to many employees. If possible, movement away from traditional eight-hour shifts, or allowing flextime for shift work, tailors an employee's work schedule to her life schedule.

Recognize the diversity of your employees by expanding your anti-discrimination policies to include areas not currently addressed by law, such as cultural profiling, sexual orientation, and gender identity.

A well-rounded benefits package that addresses the life needs of a modern workforce is your best insurance that your company will be attractive to the very best talent available. The package creates a work environment with less attrition because your employees feel both their families and themselves are protected.

The creation of the best practice benefits package, therefore, is the single most important task we can undertake as managers to ensure the success and longevity of our company.

Appraisals

Every person working with us desires feedback on how well he or she is performing. We all need that information to both grow and adapt to our responsibilities. The traditional methods of performance appraisal fail miserably here and are definitely not the best practice.

Employees are dynamic and do not fit well into defined job descriptions. While employees do possess the skills required for a particular task, the job description fails to take into account such aspects as attitude, work ethics, team spirit, and dedication. We also tend to appraise based solely on the skill sets in a written job description.

For example, let us take an employee named Joe. Among his other duties, Joe's job requires him to attend a weekly meeting and give a report on new projects, which he does. Occasionally in these meetings,

Joe has the brilliant ability to bring cohesiveness and resolution to all those in attendance when their opinions differ. Joe is a natural facilitator. This skill, however, is not part of his job description, nor does it need to be. Joe's job merely requires his attendance and reporting. In this case, to include the ability to facilitate in the job description places an unnecessary requirement on anyone who may desire the job in the future. However, if we base Joe's appraisal solely on his job description we may never capture and give credit for his valuable talent.

Employees are not square like the boxes we put them in, but more like pieces of a jigsaw puzzle. They have bumps that connect with the hollows of others, and vice versa. Despite our definition of a job, employees will naturally exhibit and act on these aspects of themselves. Like Joe, most employees will utilize talents that are not written into their job description. We must, therefore, find other ways to review job performance and reduce the dependence on the canned checklist approach. One way is to ask our fellow managers for feedback on Joe. What have they observed? Are there any actions above and beyond the call of duty? What about his attitude among his peers as well as managers? Unless you personally interact with Joe as much as anyone else, talking with the employees Joe interacts with every day gives a much better understanding of his overall performance.

Also remember this: Our responses to the standard appraisal checklist are based on personal feelings, memories, thoughts, and ideas about Joe. The thoughts most likely to surface are the ones that occurred recently, usually within the past six weeks. Do not fall into the trap of allowing your responses and Joe's appraisal to be colored by some event, good or bad, that happened recently. Instead, keep notes of *all* the things Joe has done. This does not have to be a formalized file, nor does it need to add lots of work to your day. Simply keep a log and when a notable event or observation occurs, write it down. The challenge is to be unbiased and log in all notable events, not only the bad ones. Especially make note of all the events outside Joe's job description, such as volunteering to train on another job so he can act as a temporary replacement if needed, or observe smaller groups of fellow workers who follow Joe's ideas due to his talent as a leader.

Then, when necessary, a review with Joe of this *diary* becomes Joe's appraisal. If you must have a checklist, make the diary review one of the more heavily weighted items. The remaining checklist items should be tangible, measurable items that track Joe's performance. Items such as work throughput, timeliness, first-quality yield, or tasks completed on schedule.

If you must perform formal appraisals, do not let this stop you from a daily recognition of a job well done or an opportunity to correct mistakes. Our employees want our feedback. As managers, we must train ourselves to step out of our comfort zone and applaud work well done. A sincere *pat on the back* every so often means far more than a formalized appraisal. When there are times when we must correct someone for poor performance, we must do so positively, and with the assurance that we sincerely want to help our employees get better. Nothing kills motivation and drags down attitude faster than a negatively handled employee correction. Before attempting interaction with your employees, either positively or otherwise, take a minute to think about what you are going to say, and remember the Golden Rule about treating others as you wish to be treated. Your attitude and how you handle yourself and your employees directly affects their performance. Remember that while you are appraising them, you are, in a very real way, appraising yourself.

Promotion

> Sam loved his job. Every workday for the past three years, Sam would clock in and set about his task of organizing the area around his workstation on the production line. The previous shift usually left the area in a state of disarray. Sam believed in a place for everything and everything in its place. Curiously, Sam's shift always produced at a higher rate and with greater efficiency than all the other shifts. It seems Sam's skills at organization went beyond fastidiousness; his skills created real quality and throughput differences. Fortunately, the company management became aware of Sam's skills and promoted him to a new position. Sam doesn't work on the line anymore. He now works with the Industrial Engineering group studying workflow and optimizing work areas to maximize efficiency.

Other than a paycheck and benefits, the next most desirable goal of our employees is the chance for advancement. Human beings are happier when they are in an environment of growth possibilities. Promotion into the next level of responsibility, or into a new job entirely, refreshes the mental attitude and provides stimulation. Promotion creates a happier workforce by giving employees a goal to strive for. There are two schools of thought on the process of promotion: one based on company seniority and the other on demonstrated skills. Some companies use one or the other. I believe both must be used for best practices in this area.

Simply placing the most senior person in an available slot does not mean he is the most qualified. Take, for example, an employee who has been with the company for 10 years. That employee either has 10 years of accumulated experience or 1 year of experience taken 10 times over. In other words, he never really grows or absorbs the finer details of the job; he just shows up every day and does the time. Experience is not something we can write down in a work instruction or something that can be taught. Even the best trainers can merely give information and show how to accomplish a task. They cannot give the experience of doing the job to their trainees. Experience is its own teacher.

Conversely, having a skill set does not necessarily mean the person has everything required to master the new job. Skills must be honed to fit in with the current task. The honing process happens only when sufficient understanding of the job is also present. Adaptation of skills to the job transforms those skills into something new and more specialized. The work and the knowledge required to create, and then apply, specialized skills are the pathway to experience.

So when developing your protocol for promotion, both skills and experience, including mentoring, must have equal weight. The rules and protocols on which you base your promotion decisions must be clearly communicated and transparent to your employees. All employees should receive education in the promotion process as part of the company's new hire orientation process. Job opportunities should be posted with all requirements for experience and skills clearly outlined as well as the pay scale.

You may question whether my last idea about posting the pay scale is the best practice. In my experience, I have seen hourly wage rates posted along with job opportunities while pay ranges for management salary jobs are never listed. In my opinion, this can cause suspicion among employees and create a real sense of us-versus-them. Transparency, like honesty, is always the best practice.

This posting of requirements allows potential candidates to screen themselves before applying for the new job. If we are doing a good job of appraisal, and providing constant feedback and leadership, as mentioned earlier, our employees will be aware of their strengths, weaknesses, skills, and talents. They will be able to judge for themselves whether they are a worthy candidate. This understanding of the rules and of oneself creates a smaller pool of candidates, increases our odds of connecting the right person to the right job, and bolsters employee happiness and motivation.

If at all possible, promote from within your organization. I feel nothing kills employee motivation and dedication faster than hiring from the outside for an open position. Understandably, there are times when this is unavoidable. However, we must realize that our employees desire advancement and recognition. Employees can still work their way up through the ranks to better paying positions with more responsibility. Your employees deserve a chance to grow as your company grows. If we remember to keep the employees we already have in mind, we will give them the best training, mentoring, and education possible to prepare them for the next step in their careers.

Management Visibility and Open-Door Policy

Everyone on the floor knew Mr. McKenzie, "Mr. M,"
they called him. Mr. M was the plant manager
for the entire operation His office was upstairs with large
glass windows so he could look out on the whole
manufacturing floor at once. All the employees
could see Mr. M, too. They could see him pounding his
fist while on the phone or talking face to face with other
managers, all the while displaying the anger that had
become his signature. The employees never saw Mr. M
on the shop floor, however, unless he had a really bad
problem and was looking for someone to pound on.
Therefore, no one on the floor ever had a problem or

would ever think to approach Mr. M with a suggestion
for fear of the repercussions. There was one problem Mr.
M could never figure out. Why was the employee
attrition rate higher at his site than at any other in the
company?

We previously mentioned the importance of maintaining a connection between ourselves and our employees. We are the managerial
face of our company. Our employees work best when they are able
to interact and have a dialog with us. I am not suggesting the establishment of personal relationships outside the workplace between
managers and employees. That is a dangerous practice and one that I
discourage. In the workplace, however, best practices dictate that we
are accessible to our employees. If you are a manager or supervisor,
do not stay behind your desk or isolated in your office. Get out on
the floor, walk around, and talk to your employees. Show a sincere
interest in how and what they are doing. Make it a daily point, at the
very least, to say, "Good morning" to all your employees. This same
idea applies to higher-level managers as well. Let yourself be seen on
the shop floor on some a regular basis. Dialog between all layers of
management and employees prevents the image of elusiveness and
tears down management silos.

Nothing promotes this idea of accessibility better than a published
open-door policy. The open-door policy holds that all employees may
at any time speak to their manager about any problem or issue they
are having. Each employee is encouraged to share any ideas for
improving a process, procedures, or operation of the manufacturing
site. In other words, the office door is always open for whatever dialog
the employee desires. The manager is then committed to listen, investigate, and provide feedback. If the feedback is not acceptable or is not
forthcoming in a timely fashion, the employee has the right to request
a meeting with the next highest manager. This process can continue
up the chain of management until a satisfactory answer is received.
This policy is covered with each new hire and is posted as part of the
company's policies and procedures.

Both visibility and the open door allow the vital exchange of communication. Communication is of central importance to all good relationships and at the heart of the best practices management style.

FINAL THOUGHTS

As I mentioned at the beginning of this chapter, managing our employees well requires more effort than making our products. Managing our employees can also be a very rewarding experience. Investing in the betterment of our employees, providing a level of security, and allowing our employees to flourish all help our company to flourish. Recapping our best practices, we find:

- Improve employees' chances for success through education.
- Provide the very best in job training.
- Groom employees through mentoring.
- Instill a sense of empowerment.
- Offer a comprehensive benefits package.
- Recognize and reward real-world performance.
- Promote from within when possible.
- Make yourself *managerial*.

Conclusion

We have reached the end of our journey together. I thank you for your time. We have covered a lot of ground, and many topics, most of which were just a straightforward application of good common sense or simply doing the right thing. I hope you found some tidbits that will allow you to reap benefits from the time we spent together.

Throughout this book, you have seen a common theme. In order to optimize your productivity and quality, you must be willing to constantly examine your processes and make adjustments where needed. For some companies this is a *revolutionary* idea. How often I have heard, "We've always done it this way—why change?" I answer this by saying, "The world today is in constant change. Customers want more, for less, delivered faster and free from problems." Customer's tastes are more refined and they expect not only innovative, high-quality products but a superior customer service experience. We have at our disposal today tools that were the stuff of science fiction 30 years ago. These tools allow us to know more about our systems and processes, and give us the ability to reach a global economy like never before. We *must* embrace the idea of constant examination and optimization in order to compete. You may rest assured, dear reader, that if we are not willing to put *all we do* under the microscope of best practices, there are plenty of competitors waiting in the wings ready to step in and take our place. In light of this environment, application of best practices is not optional. Best practices are not *revolutionary*. No, best practices are *evolutionary*.

It matters not whether you are a department manager or the CEO of your company. I challenge you, each day, to see your operations with a fresh set of eyes, to look for opportunities to improve, to not settle for the status quo. Go to work with the idea that *survival of the fittest* is your goal for the day. Then, take the steps, small or large, to lead the *evolution* of your company into the next version of your highest vision for it. That is what optimization is really about—vision. Where do you see yourself in five years? What steps are you taking *now* to realize that vision? That is the *attitude of best practices*.

I leave you with this final thought. With all due respect to the great philosopher, Socrates, who said, "An unexamined life is not worth living."

I say, likewise, "An unexamined process, procedure, or protocol is not worth having."

Quality Requirements Checklist

Whether you are manufacturing or buying a product, there are certain key pieces of information that are vital to building the item to your customer's needs. This same type of information is needed when specifying *your* needs to a supplier. This list is an outline of broad, generalized categories with questions that will help you create this *body of knowledge* about your particular process or requirement.

Raw Materials

- Are there restrictions on raw materials, type, supplier, or supplier/location combination?
- What certifications or requirements are needed?

Dimensional Characteristics (may be addressed by drawing or print)

- Physical dimensions, length, width, diameters, thickness, and so on, including tolerances
- Shape, pattern, angles, including tolerances
- All dimensional units of measure
- Dimensional restrictions like weight, height, length

Chemical Characteristics

- Specific gravity, pH, viscosity, and so on, including tolerances
- Hazardous material information, including Material Safety Data Sheet

External Specifications

- Are there external industry and/or military specifications or drawings required?
- Do these outside documents reference any additional documents that are also needed, such as raw material specifications?
- Have all documents, drawings, and specifications been through the internal review and approval process, and are they visible through internal information systems?
- As part of the specification review, has process capability analysis been performed on all dimensional and testing requirements? Has capability been established?
- Are there any agreed process control documents required between us and the final customer?
- If so, are said documents properly signed off by authorized officials and on file within our quality system?

Testing

- List of tests required for the final test report or certification
- List of tests for process control. These include all product characteristics, including product build, and may overlap dimensional characteristics.
- Ranges and/or targets for all testing, including tolerances
- Units of measure for all tests
- Number of tests per sample and the form of the final compliance data (e.g., raw, average, or calculated data)
- Which form of data is matched to specification for compliance?
- Are there written procedures and training in place for tests?
- Is equipment available for tests?

- Does testing need to be witnessed by outside source such as customer or government inspector?
- Are there any requirements for data retention time?

Outside Testing

- Is outside testing required?
- Do we have an established vendor?
- Has outside vendor been approved through our internal approval process?
- Does outside vendor need qualifications or accreditation?
- Outside Testing also includes all the checklist items for Testing.

Inspection

- Are documented visual or instrumental inspection standards in place, including defect definitions or pictures?
- What is the allowable defect count or severity allowed while maintaining a first-quality product? (May be zero.)
- If a defect level is allowed, which defects can remain and which must be either removed or reworked if possible?
- Does defect proximity count as a single occurrence or must all defects be counted? If single occurrence, what are the proximity boundaries (e.g., within an inch, or all on the same side)?
- Determine defect size, if allowed.
- Can some defects be categorized or rated instead of counted (e.g., good, bad, or numerical scale)?
- Are inspection/approval required by outside source like government agency or customer?
- Are there special inspection conditions like lighting or location? In process or offline?
- Are defect maps or defect marking required?
- Determine disposition criteria for all inspection points.
- Deternube inspection criteria for final packed product (e.g., damaged cartons, missing labels).

Sampling

■ What are the sampling frequency and unit of sampling for both testing and inspections? For example, may be 100 percent inspection, or sorting, or statistical sampling plan. Units may be piece, case, or lot.

■ What are the accept and reject levels for each test and inspection?

■ What is the protocol for re-sampling?

Qualification

■ Does this product need to be qualified before going to full production?

■ What sampling, testing, and reporting are required outside normal production?

■ Are there special handling and production requirements to create qualification items (such as production from a single raw material source, or items must be submitted from separate production runs)?

Interior Packaging

■ What level of protection is required (e.g., commercial, export, waterproof, moisture proof)?

■ What packaging materials are required (e.g., separators, plastic wrap, bubble wrap, paper, vapor barrier, desiccant, stretch wrap, foam, suspensions, dunnage)?

■ Is there interior packing, such as intermediate cartons?

■ Determine all packaging dimensions such as plastic thickness, separator size, or desiccant absorption limit.

■ Determine any packaging special instructions, such as requirements for heat seals, number of desiccant packs, or labeling.

■ Are there environmental disposal issues for any materials used?

Packing

■ What level of exterior packing protection is required (e.g., standard commercial practice or specialty, packing for export, weather-proofing, stretch-wrapped, etc.)?

- What type of external container is required (e.g., cartons, buckets, bags, or bundles)?
- What are the specifications, if any, on container materials (e.g., cardboard type, density, burst strength for cardboard boxes)?
- Are there environmental disposal issues for any materials used?

Labeling/Marking

- Are labels required on exterior containers, and if so, what information should they contain?
- What is the label size?
- Does the label require a special layout to an industry standard such as automotive?
- What information is required on the labels?
- Do the labels need bar coding, RFID, or other means of reading?
- Are labels also required on smaller interior packs, and if so, what information should they contain?
- What are the number and location of all labels for unit packs and final packs?
- Are there any specialty markings, labels, stenciling required, and if so, what information?

Palletization

- Is palletization of containers required?
- What are the specifications for the pallet? Details include pallet design and layout, material type (wood or other), additional treatments such as fumigation or heat treatment for exportation.
- What is the pallet loading layout? Details include units per pallet, tie sheets, stretch wrapping, container orientation, and stacking layout.
- Is pallet strapping required? Are there restricted or required materials such as steel or plastic?
- Environmental disposal issues for any materials used?

Final Reporting to External Customer

- What documentation is to be included in the information package for shipment?

- Are test reports required, and if so, which data?

- Are certifications required to external specification?

- Are defect maps required?

- Is evidence of process control required (e.g., setup sheets, control charts, operator signoff, etc.)?

- Are raw material certifications included?

- How is data reported (e.g., in raw form, or averages, by shipping lot, process lot, or individual results)?

- Is any unique product ID such as a customer part number required on documents?

- Are there restrictions for use of paper versus electronic documents and original signatures?

- Is a packing list also required linking identification of items shipped to test results?

About the Author

Bobby Hull is Corporate Systems Analyst at BGF Industries Inc., formally known as Burlington Industries, Inc., and co-founder of Questworks Productions, a company specializing in computer training, Web site design, graphic design, staff development workshops, stress reduction workshops, quality control consulting, and auditing. In his analyst position, Hull focuses on designing and implementing quality control and business intelligence solutions for various divisions of BGF Industries, a multimillion-dollar textile company.

Previous to this role, Hull spent over 10 years as a Senior Quality Engineer, coordinating all facets of the BGF quality control program, including the redesign of several quality subsystems in order to meet the requirements of ISO 9001:2000. During his more than 30 years with BGF Industries, Hull has performed in the capacity of finishing inspector, lab technician, crew leader, and manager of their QC laboratory.

Hull holds a Doctorate of Divinity from the American Institute of Holistic Theology, Birmingham, Alabama, and has completed coursework in Chemistry at the University of Richmond and in Fine Arts at Lynchburg College.

Index